**New Directions for
Institutional Research**

Robert K. Toutkoushian
EDITOR-IN-CHIEF

J. Fredericks Volkwein
ASSOCIATE EDITOR

Using Quantitative Data to Answer Critical Questions

Frances K. Stage
EDITOR

Number 133 • Spring 2007
Jossey-Bass
San Francisco

USING QUANTITATIVE DATA TO ANSWER CRITICAL QUESTIONS
Frances K. Stage (ed.)
New Directions for Institutional Research, no. 133
Robert K. Toutkoushian, Editor-in-Chief

NEW DIRECTIONS FOR INSTITUTIONAL RESEARCH (ISSN 0271-0579, electronic ISSN 1536-075X) is part of The Jossey-Bass Higher and Adult Education Series and is published quarterly by Wiley Subscription Services, Inc., A Wiley Company, at Jossey-Bass, 989 Market Street, San Francisco, California 94103-1741 (publication number USPS 098-830). Periodicals Postage Paid at San Francisco, California, and at additional mailing offices. POSTMASTER: Send address changes to New Directions for Institutional Research, Jossey-Bass, 989 Market Street, San Francisco, California 94103-1741.

SUBSCRIPTIONS cost $80.00 for individuals and $185.00 for institutions, agencies, and libraries in the United States. See order form at end of book.

EDITORIAL CORRESPONDENCE should be sent to Robert K. Toutkoushian, Educational Leadership and Policy Studies, Education 4220, 201 N. Rose Ave., Indiana University, Bloomington, IN 47405.

New Directions for Institutional Research is indexed in *College Student Personnel Abstracts, Contents Pages in Education,* and *Current Index to Journals in Education* (ERIC).

Microfilm copies of issues and chapters are available in 16mm and 35mm, as well as microfiche in 105mm, through University Microfilms, Inc., 300 North Zeeb Road, Ann Arbor, Michigan 48106-1346.

www.josseybass.com

THE ASSOCIATION FOR INSTITUTIONAL RESEARCH was created in 1966 to benefit, assist, and advance research leading to improved understanding, planning, and operation of institutions of higher education. Publication policy is set by its Publications Committee.

For information about the Association for Institutional Research, write to the following address:

AIR Executive Office
114 Stone Building
Florida State University
Tallahassee, FL 32306-4462

(850) 644-4470

air@mailer.fsu.edu
http://airweb.org

CONTENTS

THE WILEY BICENTENNIAL—KNOWLEDGE FOR GENERATIONS

*E*ach generation has its unique needs and aspirations. When Charles Wiley first opened his small printing shop in lower Manhattan in 1807, it was a generation of boundless potential searching for an identity. And we were there, helping to define a new American literary tradition. Over half a century later, in the midst of the Second Industrial Revolution, it was a generation focused on building the future. Once again, we were there, supplying the critical scientific, technical, and engineering knowledge that helped frame the world. Throughout the 20th Century, and into the new millennium, nations began to reach out beyond their own borders and a new international community was born. Wiley was there, expanding its operations around the world to enable a global exchange of ideas, opinions, and know-how.

For 200 years, Wiley has been an integral part of each generation's journey, enabling the flow of information and understanding necessary to meet their needs and fulfill their aspirations. Today, bold new technologies are changing the way we live and learn. Wiley will be there, providing you the must-have knowledge you need to imagine new worlds, new possibilities, and new opportunities.

Generations come and go, but you can always count on Wiley to provide you the knowledge you need, when and where you need it!

WILLIAM J. PESCE
PRESIDENT AND CHIEF EXECUTIVE OFFICER

PETER BOOTH WILEY
CHAIRMAN OF THE BOARD

EDITOR'S NOTES

In this volume, we describe what is an increasingly evident way of conducting quantitative research. This approach does not seek merely to verify models but, in addition, to question and then modify models, or to create new models that better describe the ever-differentiating individuals who are the focus of educational research.

We examine a variety of higher education issues from a critical stance, using quantitative methods. We demonstrate ways of moving beyond traditional conceptualizations of quantitative research and use our scholarship to push the boundaries of what we know by questioning mainstream notions of higher education through the examination of policies, the reframing of theories and measures, and the reexamination of traditional questions for nontraditional populations. Although the work presented here is divergent, the commonality of the presentations lies in each scholar's critical approach to conventional quantitative scholarship. We hope to demonstrate that being a *quantitative criticalist* comes with the questions we ask, not with the methods we use to answer them.

The chapters that follow provide perspectives on critical quantitative research and demonstrate how these analyses add to the discourse questioning some of the assumptions of traditional quantitative approaches.

In the first chapter, I invoke various scholars' definitions of critical inquiry, and relying primarily on Kincheloe and McLaren (1994), I provide arguments to justify taking the discourse beyond questions of method. Next I provide examples of the work of *quantitative criticalists* in higher education, and then describe more fully the characteristics of this approach vis-à-vis current dominant research paradigms. Finally, I provide a brief overview of my own research on students' participation in mathematics and science-based majors as I've moved from a postpositivist to a quantitative criticalist.

In Chapter Two, Ben Baez asks how educational research is or can be *critically transformative*. He defines the term *critical* for us and explores the extent to which educational research can offer critiques of our world that allow us to transform it. Because quantitative research is not usually thought about as providing such critique he helps us think about that which we call critical. He ends by suggesting that we judge whether or not research is critical by evaluating the questions asked and the critiques offered.

In Chapter Three, scholars Deborah Faye Carter and Sylvia Hurtado begin by discussing the influence of autobiography on scholarship, particularly for quantitative research. Next they provide illustration using their

NEW DIRECTIONS FOR INSTITUTIONAL RESEARCH, no. 133, Spring 2007 © Wiley Periodicals, Inc.
Published online in Wiley InterScience (www.interscience.wiley.com) • DOI: 10.1002/ir.199

own work, then explore key research questions and dilemmas that researchers face in critical work. Finally, they suggest potential solutions.

In Chapter Four, Robert Teranishi describes how the use of between-group approaches in quantitative research on race can limit what we know about educational experiences, opportunities, and outcomes of individual racial groups. He presents examples to illustrate misrepresentation of educational success for Asian and Pacific Islander Americans in quantitative data. Finally, he uses his own research focusing on Asian American students in U.S. higher education to demonstrate that critical research frameworks in quantitative research can yield important and interesting perspectives. These analyses can be applied to the study of other racial groups to improve what we know about subpopulations in broader racial categories.

Laura Perna begins Chapter Five by discussing the importance of studying the underrepresentation of blacks and Hispanics in American higher education. She then describes a traditional conceptual model for examining racial and ethnic group differences in college enrollment. She points out the strengths inherent in using quantitative analyses to address the question and examines challenges that quantitative researchers will face as well. Perna closes with recommendations for the use of quantitative analyses of an integrated conceptual model to gain additional insights into gaps in college enrollment for specific groups.

Next, in Chapter Six, Edward St. John describes what he calls a *critical-empirical approach* to the study of college access. He explores the role of policy researchers in seeking educational equity. He contrasts his approach with the scientific approach most commonly advocated in educational research. He describes his social justice framework, which has evolved from his work, and provides a case study of the influence of educational policy on access to higher education. He concludes with guidance for other researchers.

In Chapter Seven Jillian Kinzie introduces a research project conceptualized and conducted from a critical and feminist perspective. She examines women's participation in mathematics and science-based majors. But by ignoring a traditional assumption about the way students behave, she is able to demonstrate a new possibility for student participation. She elaborates on her critical approach and discusses how that approach influenced the development of her research questions, data analysis, interpretation, and presentation of findings.

In the final chapter, I discuss some of the technical reasons that probabilistic research, in the ways it is often conducted using traditional assumptions, masks the experiences of many participants in education. I present tasks that must be addressed to move higher education from a state of complacency to a dynamic questioning discipline. I close with recommendations for those who wish to incorporate critical perspectives into their own quantitative work as well as for those who wish to read it both critically and appreciatively.

New Directions for Institutional Research • DOI: 10.1002/ir

Much of our work can be described as theory development, or even theory disconfirmation. Some of the work in this volume's chapters focuses on criticism of educational systems or policy. We believe it is important to point out weaknesses in educational systems, educational theories, and educational analysis, and we do so in the work presented here. We must put all our resources into critical higher education work—all our approaches and our variety of conceptualizations have a contribution to make. Work reported here can be viewed as example for those who seek to move their own research agendas beyond the expected. All we ask is that you read our work with an open mind regarding what you might learn.

Frances K. Stage
Editor

Reference

Kincheloe, J. L., and McLaren, P. L. "Rethinking Critical Theory and Qualitative Research." In N. K. Denzin and Y. S. Lincoln (eds.), *Handbook of Qualitative Research* (pp. 138–157). Thousand Oaks, Calif.: Sage, 1994.

FRANCES KING STAGE is professor of administration, leadership, and technology in the Steinhardt School at New York University and a former Senior Fellow at the National Science Foundation.

1

Drawing on the work of several prominent scholars, the author describes the evolution of quantitative critical inquiry and compares this perspective to traditional research paradigms.

Answering Critical Questions Using Quantitative Data

Frances K. Stage

With this volume we seek to demonstrate the ways that we as scholars turn our quantitative skills toward asking and answering critical questions in higher education research. We examine a variety of higher education issues from a critical stance, using quantitative methods. Collectively, our work demonstrates ways of moving beyond traditional conceptualizations of quantitative research. We use our scholarship to push the boundaries of what we know by questioning mainstream notions of higher education through the examination of policies, the reframing of theories and measures, and the reexamination of traditional questions for nontraditional populations. Although the work presented here is divergent, the commonality of the presentations lies in each scholar's critical approach to conventional quantitative scholarship.

In the following chapters the authors focus on research questions rather than methods or findings. They describe the ways conventional research drove them to the questions of their studies, and then tell how those results challenged the status quo. Because the perspective of this volume is on the framing of the research questions, methods and results are secondary and are presented only to illustrate various applications of critical quantitative inquiry. We hope to demonstrate that being a *quantitative criticalist* comes with the questions we ask, not with the methods we use to answer them.

In this chapter, I invoke various scholars' definitions of critical inquiry, and relying primarily on Kincheloe and McLaren (1994), provide arguments

NEW DIRECTIONS FOR INSTITUTIONAL RESEARCH, no. 133, Spring 2007 © Wiley Periodicals, Inc.
Published online in Wiley InterScience (www.interscience.wiley.com) • DOI: 10.1002/ir.200

to justify taking the discourse beyond discussions of method. Next I provide examples of the work of several prominent *quantitative criticalists* in higher education, and then describe more fully the characteristics of this approach vis-à-vis current dominant research paradigms. Finally, I provide a brief overview of my own research on students' participation in mathematics and science-based majors as I've moved from being a postpositivist to a quantitative criticalist.

Critical Theory

Critical theory evolved from the German Frankfurt school and was described by Habermas (1971) as differing in aim, structure, and justification from "quantitative" (described as empirical-analytic) science, which is designed to predict and control natural events. Tierney and Rhoads (1993) described critical theorists as those who (1) seek to understand the experiences of individuals and groups in light of cultural constraints and societal prescriptions; (2) recognize the importance that power plays in structuring human subjectivity; (3) give credence to the importance of cultural difference; (4) investigate how science and knowledge get defined and changed; and (5) extend theory into the arena of action.

Schwandt (1997) described critical social science as characterized by five general themes. First, it aims to integrate theory and practice so that individuals are aware of inconsistencies and contradictions between their belief systems and social practices. Second, critical social science rejects the idea of a detached social scientist and "is oriented toward social and individual transformation" (p. 24). Third, critical social science rejects traditional empirical research schemes, which aim to eliminate crises, conflict, and critique. Critical social science embraces practical, moral, and ethically and politically informed research. Fourth, critical social inquiry requires enlightened self-knowledge and effective social political action. Finally, critical social research examines possibility and transformation as outcomes of the research.

Kincheloe and McLaren (1994) present the project of critical research as interrogation "in order to uncover the contradictions and negations embodied in any objective description" and to discover the "hidden assumptions . . . the critical researcher must dig out and expose" (p. 144). The other authors in this volume and I claim that such descriptions do not preclude the possibility of quantitative approaches. In addition, we believe that as quantitative researchers we are uniquely able to find those contradictions and negative assumptions that exist in quantitative research frames.

Although the majority of critical work in higher education is conducted by scholars who apply naturalistic and qualitative techniques to answer questions, well-known scholars outside higher education promote the use of data and numbers in critical work, such as Carspecken (1996) and Comstock (1982). Even Karl Marx (1999) employed quantitative analysis in his socialist arguments (see *Das Kapital*). As a group, the authors in this volume hope to refute claims that quantitative analysis is always formulaic, reductive, and instrumental in approach. Rather, we demonstrate that working with data in the form of numbers can make a contribution to critical inquiry in higher education.

To structure the argument, I chose Kincheloe and McLaren's (1994) definition of critical theory. Their definition stresses underlying commonalities of definitions that they caution should not imply consensus. For example, Lather's (1992) definition of critical inquiry most often includes inquiry into how lives are mediated by classism, racism, sexism, and heterosexism but assumes qualitative approaches to those questions. Kincheloe and McLaren's definition is appealing because they avoid methodological assumptions that would preclude the reason for this volume, and they seek a consensual definition of critical theory.

Briefly, Kincheloe and McLaren (1994) describe as *critical* a researcher or theorist who attempts to use his or her work as a form of social or cultural criticism and who accepts the following paraphrased assumptions:

- Thought is mediated by socially and historically created power relations.
- Facts cannot be isolated from values.
- The relationship between concept and object is never fixed and is often socially mediated.
- Language is central to the formation of subjectivity.
- Certain groups in society hold privilege over others that is maintained if subordinates accept their status as natural.
- Oppression has many faces that must be examined simultaneously.
- Mainstream research practices generally reproduce class, race, and gender oppression.

The seven elements of Kincheloe and McLaren's (1994) definition, although broad and consensus seeking, do not preclude quantitative interrogations of these issues.

In fact, many researchers in higher education use quantitative means to "attempt to confront the injustice of a society or a sphere within the society" (Kincheloe and McLaren, 1994, p. 140) and to demonstrate class, race, and gender oppression using numbers. For example, Glazer-Raymo (2005) used numbers to demonstrate inequities for women in academe, and Slaughter and Rhoades (2004) used quantitative approaches to illuminate the monetary buildup of technology and "big science" at the expense of the social sciences and the humanities in higher education.

Further, Kincheloe and McLaren enjoin researchers to become self-conscious, a noble aspiration for quantitative researchers. With heightened awareness, who better to discover "ideological imperatives" and "epistemological presuppositions" as well as "subjective, intersubjective, and normative reference claims" than those who see the direct results of those claims in their everyday work (Kincheloe and McLaren, 1994, p. 140).

Recently scholars have written in more inclusive terms across the quantitative and qualitative paradigms. For example, Tashakkori and Teddlie (1998) write of a pragmatist paradigm that argues against dominant philosophies and rejects the "forced choice" between qualitative and quantitative approaches. They acknowledge the value-laden nature of research, that fact is theory-laden, and that the nature of reality is constructed. Research approaches are viewed as part and parcel of an eclectic tool kit, wherein the researcher hunts for the tool to fit the question.

In contrast, the *quantitative criticalist*, rather than confirming conventional wisdoms and seeking consensus, adapts a proactive stance by consciously choosing questions that seek to challenge. The quantitative criticalist seeks to forge challenges, illuminate conflict, and develop critique through quantitative methods in an effort to move theory, knowledge, and policy to a higher plane.

Quantitative Possibility

According to critical theorists, the project of critical theory is not merely the rewriting of the world but also "posing the research itself as a set of ideological practices" (Kincheloe and McLaren, 1994, p. 144). Indeed, without broad questioning of ideological practices, the need for rewriting would be an endless duplicitous task. One group of theorists and researchers would continually produce work that the second group of theorists would then examine for flaws and refutations.

Kincheloe and McLaren (1994) enjoin that "[e]mpirical analysis needs to be interrogated in order to uncover the contradictions and negations embodied in any objective description" (p. 144). But who better to help uncover the "ideological inscriptions" in quantitative research than quantitative analysts themselves? As an example, recently John Braxton (2000) edited a book focused on challenges and revisions to a widely used theoretical model in higher education, the Tinto model of college student persistence. Two dozen scholars with years of research suggested additions and modifications based on their successes, failures, and discoveries using that model. This book can serve as an example for future conference symposia, reports, and books questioning assumptive practices and generating possible alternatives .

Consider the following possibilities:

- A graduate student observes underlying assumptions in sociological causal models. She notices that by failing to take into account family income, empirical research consistently problematized (stigmatized?) single motherhood. Her quantitative dissertation controls for income to examine the relationships of single motherhood and single fatherhood to various educational and social benchmarks for children.

- Two researchers notice in their own research that traditional causal models of college student satisfaction and retention do not help explain the college experiences of immigrant students. In interpretive studies of immigrant college students' experiences, they read about the demoralizing effects of campus racism. They design a quantitative study that includes indicators of racism resulting in a more clear understanding of immigrant students' satisfaction and persistence.

These hypothetical examples are not unlike the origins of some quantitative research being conducted today. Increasingly, researchers do not need to have a personal sociocultural stake in outcomes (although they sometimes do) in order to recognize erroneous assumptions and ideological traps. Enlightened quantitative researchers are often better able to uncover the "hidden assumptions" and "ideological inscriptions" in their own work, as well as in the quantitative work of others. Researchers inexperienced in quantitative approaches might not recognize or understand the detailed measurement of some variables, the effects of ignoring other variables, and the implications of positional placements of variables in causal models.

This volume describes an increasingly evident way of conducting quantitative research. This approach does not seek merely to verify models. Rather it focuses on questioning and then modifying models or creating new models that better describe the ever-differentiating individuals who are the focus of educational research. When models do not accurately reflect a given population's experiences, the task is to pose alternatives to those models. Rather than focus on explanation, or fairness, it focuses on equity concerns that can often be highlighted through analysis of large data sets—for example, by focusing on differences by race, class, and gender.

Table 1.1 depicts a familiar comparison between critical and positivist approaches. As we can see, critical quantitative research falls between the two. If we focus solely on research methods—arguably the less interesting of a researcher's concerns—we see little difference between the positivistic approach and the critical quantitative approach. However, the second part of the table, the most interesting part, rests with the motivation for the research.

For the critical quantitative researcher, characteristics of method, the top half of the table—scope, findings, focus, data, and kinds of results reported—resemble typical positivistic research. The scope is broad rather than in-depth, the findings are generalizable using aggregated data, and the results are independent of context. However, it is in the motivation for the research, as illustrated in the lower half of the table, that the questions, goals, and outcomes of the research more closely match those of the critical researcher.

The critical researcher calls into question models, assumptions, and measures traditionally made under the positivist perspective. By using techniques such as interviews and observations, traditional critical researchers demonstrate situations and populations for whom the assumptions and models are

Table 1.1. Methods and Motivations for Research Paradigms

	Critical	Critical Quantitative	Positivist-Postpositivist
Research methods			
Scope	In-depth	Broad	Broad
Findings	Interpretive	Generalizable	Generalizable
Focus	Individual	Group	Group
Data	Idiographic	Aggregate	Aggregate
Results	Context dependent	Context independent	Context independent
Research motivation			
Questions	Model questioning	Model questioning	Model verification
		modification	confirmation
Goals	Description	Investigation	Explanation
Outcomes	Equity	Equity	Fairness

[Handwritten annotations: "model development" under Critical Questions; "Immediate" next to Goals; "Long term goal"; "change w/in or w/out current frame"; "change w/in current frame"; "clarify about current frame"]

fallacious. The critical quantitative researcher also questions models and assumptions but uses analysis of sociological and economic processes to demonstrate that for particular population groups, some widely accepted models and assumptions are inaccurate.

A positivistic researcher seeks models that nearly completely explain phenomena of interest, aiming for confirmation and verification to explain universal human behavior. But because much of positivistic research is based on previously developed models, the outcomes tend to replicate the status quo and verify meritocratic fairness. In contrast, the goal of the critical researcher is exploration or investigation. Does the model hold for a new population of interest—for example, students at urban institutions or rural, working-class students? The outcomes for any critical researcher, no matter the method, center around equity.

The critical quantitative researcher has two tasks:

- *Use data to represent educational processes and outcomes on a large scale to reveal inequities and to identify social or institutional perpetuation of systematic inequities in such processes and outcomes.* This work has become increasingly possible during the past two decades as a result of the proliferation of large representative databases, both national and institutional, broadened access to them, and the development of myriad analysis approaches.
- *Question the models, measures, and analytic practices of quantitative research in order to offer competing models, measures, and analytic practices that better describe experiences of those who have not been adequately represented.*

NEW DIRECTIONS FOR INSTITUTIONAL RESEARCH • DOI: 10.1002/ir

This task focuses on professional self-regulation and requires that quantitative researchers become less polite and more critical of themselves and their colleagues. It requires the development of inquiry focused on all aspects of quantitative research, questioning the status quo on approaches to problems and actively seeking to constantly improve the state of the art, including models, measures, and the application of analytic methods.

Some Examples

Amaury Nora and Alberto Cabrera have spent most of their careers working on expanded models of college student success. One joint effort included students' perceptions of prejudice on the parts of faculty and staff, and incidents of being singled out as different in a specific class. Their model demonstrated the importance of these new factors in persistence models for both minority and nonminority students in college (Nora and Cabrera, 1996). Among other contributions they have made are the alteration of traditional models of persistence to include ability to pay (Cabrera, 1987) and specific campus-based financial aid factors (Nora, 1990).

After exploring aspects of Latino students' sense of belonging and campus involvement through causal modeling, Sylvia Hurtado and Deborah Carter (1997) found that important aspects of involvement differed from those typically described for mainstream students. They cited the importance of transitions to college and perceptions of campus racism and suggested more careful attention to the meanings of campus involvement as modes of college attendance evolve, such as service learning, part-time attendance, and distance education. In addition, Hurtado (2001) has explored the influence of diverse classrooms on the academic development of all students, and Carter (1999) has studied the effect of institutional environments on college students' aspirations and degree expectations.

David Drew's (1996) *Aptitude Revisited* examined educational issues surrounding mathematics and science education in the United States. Along with his discursive evaluation, he provided examples of what might be considered critical quantitative analysis to help us understand what seems to be a predominantly U.S. emphasis on aptitude that systematically screens women and minorities from careers and educational opportunities.

Finally, Bensimon, Polkinghorne, Bauman, and Vallejo (2004) describe a "practitioner-as-researcher" approach that distances the research process from the academic sphere and situates it in the surroundings being studied. In their model, practitioners in the institutional environment of interest (faculty and administrators) develop research questions, decide on data to be collected, and provide analysis of results, with the advice of professional researchers. Research conducted in this fashion is certainly critical and often quantitative; it provides the data deemed most relevant in answering the questions asked in the context being studied.

These researchers described above did not merely seek to explain and predict. They studied college students knowing that college programs, counseling and advising, and even faculty behaviors were guided by quantitative research of the past. They attempted to show that by basing work in the college setting on research conducted on the students of the past, scholars may have ignored critical elements of the college experience that would promote equal educational opportunity for all students on campus.

In using quantitative methods to examine issues surrounding mathematics during the transition from high school to college, to examine nuances of college choice for low-income students, or to explore experiences of students of color in nonselective institutions, researchers can show pervasive negative effects that result from assumptions about students and about access to college and to education. The qualitative studies provide details on how subtle experiences color students' lives; the quantitative studies provide the persuasion of numbers. When the two are taken together, the critical work of educational researchers is more complete.

One Researcher's Evolution

My own earliest quantitative critical work began in the late 1980s with studies of students' participation in mathematics and science-based majors. A common practice at the time was to include the predictor variables gender and ethnicity in models of student experiences. As predictors, those variables, when significant, signaled a difference, but they did not really provide a picture of that difference. Several results led me to ask what exactly *were* the different experiences that caused race and gender to be significant? By separating groups by race and gender for analysis, my colleagues and I were able to describe patterns of experiences for specific groups of students that led to the outcomes on which we were focused—in this case participation in mathematics and science majors.

We discovered that models for predicting participation worked better for some students than others (Maple and Stage, 1991). In other words, for some student groups there were a greater number of significant predictors and greater amounts of variance explained even when we controlled for sample size. However, with our complicated models, we did not always get the results we expected and often were unable to explain our findings.

In the mid-1990s we used the National Educational Longitudinal Study of 1988 (NELS:88) database and focused on some standard college choice models widely used at the time (Hamrick and Stage, 1998). Here we first examined a conventional model for eighth graders in all schools; then for eighth graders at urban, low-income schools; then for white, Hispanic, and African American students at those low-income schools. Controlling for sample size, we were able to demonstrate that the model described college choice best for students who did not attend urban low-income schools and least well for African American students at the urban low-income schools.

NEW DIRECTIONS FOR INSTITUTIONAL RESEARCH • DOI: 10.1002/ir

We modified the college choice model based on literature from our colleagues (Attinasi, 1989; Levine and Nidiffer, 1996; McDonough, 1997; Terenzini and others, 1994). The new model included the influence of school activities and educational mentors outside the school context. The modified model actually showed improved fit for white students but little difference for students of color (Hamrick and Stage, 2004). A limitation may be the way those variables were measured and a tentative conclusion was that if such models of college choice continue to be used, they be reconceptualized independently by racial-ethnic and class groups.

Work in the late 1990s refocused on student participation in math and science-based majors (Kinzie, Stage, and Muller, 1998). This time a logistic regression model combined conventional predictors with measures of social capital. Using male and female African American, and white subgroups, we found that four of five conventional predictors were significant for white males and females and none were significant for African American males. For other African American female, Asian American and Hispanic subgroups, conventional predictors were significant until the social capital predictors were added to the model. In other words, family background was more important than prior educational experiences in explaining student success.

More recently, my work with colleagues focused on tracking of students into academic or nonacademic course work in high school. Counseling high school students into academic, vocational, or general course tracks has been practiced for decades, despite controversy (Oakes, 1988). Some defend tracking, whereas others believe it promotes systematic discrimination. Researchers have found that underrepresented minorities, low-income students, and women are less likely to study college preparatory mathematics than are white men with the same levels of high school achievement (Drew, 1996; Harris, 2000). Furthermore, these discrepancies can be the result of persuasion on the part of influential teachers and counselors or simply because of the provision of narrower curricular choices (Drew, 1996; Oakes, 1988). We explored the question: Is academic tracking in high school mathematics courses useful in helping students succeed?

In our initial study we examined relationships among students' ethnicity, course-taking patterns, and academic achievement in mathematics (Stage, Carter, and Musoba, 2003). Using data from the National Education Longitudinal Study of 1988, we divided students by racial-ethnic grouping and by quartiles according to their mathematics achievement in eighth grade. Levels of rigor in mathematics curriculum and achievement in twelfth grade were then examined. Between ethnic groups, we found significant differences in placement for students of similar levels of initial achievement. For all ethnic groups, regardless of initial mathematics achievement, a more rigorous academic curriculum resulted in significantly higher gains in achievement scores from the eighth grade to the twelfth grade. The differences were most dramatic for students with the lowest initial achievement. Current work includes foci in two directions: an analysis of the effects of tracking across racial-ethnic groups controlling for gender and socioeconomic status and an in-depth focus on the effects of academic tracking on mathematics achievement for African American men and women.

Beginning in the late 1990s I joined with other colleagues, including several of the authors contributing to this volume, at annual meetings of the Association for the Study of Higher Education to begin exploring critical quantitative possibilities and implications for our collective work (Stage, Rhoads, Bensimon, and Creswell, 1997; Stage, Hurtado, Braxton, and St. John, 2001; Stage and others, 2002). In her 2006 address to the Association for the Study of Higher Education, President Estela Bensimon enjoined scholars to question their assumptions and to conduct research that is relevant to their stakeholders. We have continued our evolution as quantitative criticalists and some of that work is detailed in the chapters of this volume.

I persist in this line of study despite a bias with which some view quantitative work. By default, as a quantitative researcher, we are sometimes viewed as theory confirmers, believers in a grand plan, incrementalists. But although I generally value quantitative inquiry, I view it with the healthy skepticism it deserves. All our approaches and our variety of conceptualizations have a contribution to make in critical higher education work. I hope you join me in incorporating critical perspectives into your own work, whether it is quantitative or qualitative.

References

Attinasi, L. "Mexican Americans' Perceptions of University Attendance and the Implications for Freshman Year Persistence." *Journal of Higher Education,* 1989, *60,* 247–277.

Bensimon, E. "The Underestimated Significance of Practitioner Knowledge in the Scholarship on Student Success." Presidential address to the Association for the Study of Higher Education, Anaheim, Calif., Nov. 2006.

Bensimon, E., Polkinghorne, D., Bauman, G., and Vallejo, E. "Doing Research That Makes a Difference." *Journal of Higher Education,* 2004, *75*(1).

Braxton, J. (ed.). *Rethinking the Departure Puzzle: New Theory and Research on College Student Retention.* Nashville: Vanderbilt University Press, 2000.

Cabrera, A. *Ability to Pay and College Persistence.* Madison: University of Wisconsin, 1987.

Carspecken, P. F. *Critical Ethnography in Educational Research: A Theoretical and Practical Guide.* New York: Routledge, 1996.

Carter, D. F. "The Impact of Institutional Choice and Environments on African-American and White Students' Degree Expectations." *Research in Higher Education,* 1999, *40*(1), 17–41.

Comstock, D. E. "A Method for Critical Research." In E. Bredo and W. Feinberg (eds.), *Knowledge and Values in Social and Educational Research.* Philadelphia: Temple University Press, 1982.

Drew, D. *Aptitude Revisited: Rethinking Math and Science Education for America's Next Century.* Baltimore: Johns Hopkins University Press, 1996.

Glazer-Raymo, J. "Professionalizing Graduate Education: The Master's Degree in the Marketplace." *ASHE Higher Education Report,* *31*(4). San Francisco: Jossey-Bass, 2005.

Habermas, J. *Knowledge and Human Interests: Theory and Practice, Communication, and the Evolution of Society.* (J. Shapiro, trans.). London: Heinemann, 1971.

Hamrick, F. A., and Stage, F. K. "High Minority Enrollment, High School Lunch Rates: Predisposition to College." *Review of Higher Education,* 1998, *21*(4), 343–357.

Hamrick, F., and Stage, F. K. "Community Activities, Educational Mentors, and College Predisposition Decisions of White, African American, and Hispanic Students." *Review of Higher Education,* 2004, *27*(2).

Harris, D. M. "Race and Track Placement: A Multilevel Analysis." Paper presented at the American Educational Research Association, Doctoral Awardee Conference, Oct. 2000.

Hurtado, S. "Linking Diversity and Educational Purpose: How Diversity Affects the Classroom Environment and Student Development." In G. Orfield (ed.), *Diversity Challenged: Evidence on the Impact of Affirmative Action.* Cambridge, Mass.: Harvard Education Publishing Group, 2001.

Hurtado, S., and Carter, D. F. "Effects of College Transition and Perceptions of Campus Racial Climate on Latino College Students' Sense of Belonging." *Sociology of Education,* 1997, *70,* 324–345.

Kincheloe, J. L., and McLaren, P. L. "Rethinking Critical Theory and Qualitative Research." In N. K. Denzin and Y. S. Lincoln (eds.), *Handbook of Qualitative Research* (pp. 138–157). Thousand Oaks, Calif.: Sage, 1994.

Kinzie, J., Stage, F., and Muller, P. "Science, Mathematics, and Engineering Majors: Cultural Capital, Aspirations, and Psychological Factors." Paper presented at the annual meeting of the American Educational Research Association, San Diego, Apr. 1998.

Lather, P. "Critical Frames in Educational Research: Feminist and Post-Structural Perspectives." *Theory into Practice, 31*(2), 1992.

Levine, A., and Nidiffer, J. *Beating the Odds: How the Poor Get to College.* San Francisco: Jossey-Bass, 1996.

Maple, S. A., and Stage, F. K. "Math/Science Major Choice: The Influence of Family Background and High School Experience by Gender and Ethnicity." *American Educational Research Journal,* 1991, *28*(1), 37–60.

Marx, K. *Das Kapital.* (reprint ed.) New York: Gateway Editions, 1999.

McDonough, P. M. *Choosing Colleges: How Social Class and Schools Structure Opportunity.* Albany: State University of New York Press, 1997.

Nora, A. "Campus-Based Aid Programs as Determinants of Retention Among Hispanic Community College Students." *Journal of Higher Education,* 1990, *61*(3), 312–331.

Nora, A., and Cabrera, A. "The Role of Perceptions of Prejudice and Discrimination on the Adjustment of Minority Students in College." *Journal of Higher Education,* 1996, *67*(2), 119–148.

Oakes, J. "Tracking in Mathematics and Science Education: A Structural Contribution to Unequal Schooling." In L. Weis (ed.), *Class, Race, and Gender in American Education.* Albany: State University of New York Press, 1988.

Schwandt, T. A. *Qualitative Inquiry: A Dictionary of Terms.* Thousand Oaks, Calif.: Sage, 1997.

Slaughter, S., and Rhoades, G. *Academic Capitalism and the New Economy: Markets, State, and Higher Education.* Baltimore: Johns Hopkins University Press, 2004.

Stage, F. K., Carter, H., and Musoba, G. "Mathematics Achievement: Early Achievement, Gender, and Course-Taking Patterns." Paper presented at the annual meeting of the American Educational Research Association, Chicago, Apr. 2003.

Stage, F. K., Hurtado, S., Braxton, J., and St. John, E. "Limitations of Probabilistic Research in the Study of College Students." Paper presented at the Association for the Study of Higher Education, Richmond, Va., Nov. 2001.

Stage, F. K., Rhoads, R., Bensimon, E., and Creswell, J. "Critical Quantitative Research: Oxymoron or Useful Perspective?" Paper presented at the Association for the Study of Higher Education, Albuquerque, Nov. 1997.

Stage, F. K., and others. "Using Quantitative Data to Answer Critical Questions." Paper presented at the Association for the Study of Higher Education, Sacramento, Nov. 2002.

Tashakkori, A., and Teddlie, C. *Mixed Methodology: Combining Qualitative and Quantitative Approaches.* Vol. 46. Thousand Oaks, Calif.: Sage, 1998.

Terenzini, P. T., and others. *The Transition to College: Diverse Students, Diverse Stories.* Chicago: Association for Institutional Research Forum, 1994.

Tierney, W. G., and Rhoads, R. A. *Higher Education: Handbook of Theory and Research.* New York: Agathon Press, 1993.

FRANCES K. STAGE is professor of administration, leadership, and technology in the Steinhardt School at New York University and a former Senior Fellow at the National Science Foundation.

NEW DIRECTIONS FOR INSTITUTIONAL RESEARCH • DOI: 10.1002/ir

2

Research should be judged by the questions asked and the critiques offered.

Thinking Critically About the "Critical": Quantitative Research as Social Critique

Benjamin Baez

> The philosophers have only *interpreted* the world, in various ways; the point, however, is to *change* it.
> —Karl Marx

I have been reading lately a great deal about educational research. It seems that quantitative approaches still are predominant (see Creswell, Goodchild, and Turner, 1996). But there seems to be a backlash of sorts against such predominance, especially over the last twenty years or so, by researchers emphasizing more or less constructivist versions of reality. These researchers emphasize qualitative and ethnographic approaches (see Schwandt, 1994; Wolcott, 1988). Thus, there has been much critique of educational research, most of it taking the form of polemics about the (a) methodologies used by researchers (see, for example, Eisner, 1997; Mayer, 2000, 2001; Barone, 2001); (b) paradigms undergirding the study of humans (see, for example, Constas, 1998a, 1998b; Guba and Lincoln, 1994; Mayer, 2000); and (c) purposes to which educational research should be put to use (examples of the latter critique are those polemics arguing that research should be directed at policymakers rather than at a small group of academics) (see Altbach, 1998; Conrad, 1989; Keller, 1998; Tierney, 2000; Willinsky, 2001).

NEW DIRECTIONS FOR INSTITUTIONAL RESEARCH, no. 133, Spring 2007 © Wiley Periodicals, Inc.
Published online in Wiley InterScience (www.interscience.wiley.com) • DOI: 10.1002/ir.201

These critiques of research get at important concerns about the best ways to address educational problems, the nature of truth, and the use to which research is put. Yet it seems to me that many scholars choose to reduce such complicated concerns to simplistic methodological questions. Such questions had seemed irrelevant to me because they failed to address adequately what it is researchers think they are doing when they claim to research anything. Those kinds of questions, as Marx suggests in the epigraph (from "Theses of Feuerbach," 1959) seem to reflect concerns over *correct* interpretations of educational problems, all the while missing a significant point: Do those interpretations allow us to change what we see is a problem in education? How is educational research *political* in that way?

So, I was pondering such concerns about educational research when Frances Stage asked me to participate on a panel for the 2002 annual meeting of the Association for the Study of Higher Education in Sacramento, California. The panel was titled "Using Quantitative Data to Answer Critical Questions." Not being a quantitative researcher, I assumed that my contribution to the panel would be limited to the "to Answer Critical Questions" part of the topic. I felt before the panel that I did not know what to say because I did not have an object, a specific issue to draw on. But as I thought more about it, I realized that I could link my concerns about educational research with the topic of this panel. And thus my focus became clearer. I wanted us to ask how research in higher education is or can be *critically transformative*—that is, to what extent educational research can offer critiques of our world that allow us to transform it. But quantitative research is not usually thought of as providing such critique, or at least not lately. So this panel, and this edition of the *New Directions* series, provided stages for thinking about that which we call *critical*.

What is *critical*? The Oxford English Dictionary (1989) defines the term, among other things, as (a) "given to judging; especially given to adverse or unfavorable criticism"; (b) "involving or exercising careful judgment or observation"; (c) "occupied with or skillful in criticism"; (d) "belonging or relating to criticism." *Criticism* is defined by that dictionary as (a) "the action of criticizing or passing judgment upon the qualities or merits of anything; especially the passing of unfavorable judgment"; (b) the "art of estimating the quality and character of literary or artistic work"; (c) the "function or work of a critic"; (d) "an act of criticizing; a critical remark, comment; a critical essay; critique."

So being *critical*, according to this dictionary view, is simply "judging" something. This seems a good start toward an understanding of quantitative research as critical, but it is not quite right for our purposes because it says nothing about what *kind* of judgment is relevant. Indeed, the term *critical* has come to mean more than just judgment, and so we must go beyond mere dictionary definitions and attempt to understand the term's cultural significance. Williams in *Keywords* (1983) suggests that a significant development of the terms *criticism, critic,* and *critical* is the assumption of an authoritative, abstract, objective (that is, non-neutral) judgment as the predominant and even natural process. Yet, in being constituted by particular authorities and invested with the legitimacy of abstraction and objectivity, the terms are political while masking the political arrangements that authorize an action as *criticism,* someone as *critic,* and something as *critical.* That which we call critical takes place in particular political contexts, and so what needs to be "understood is the specificity of the response, which is not an abstract 'judgment' but even where including, as often necessarily, positive or negative responses, a definite practice, in active and complex relationship with its whole situation and context" (p. 86). This seems to me to be a roundabout way of saying that the idea of *critical* must be understood in particular contexts, and such understanding has to recognize the politics and political arrangements associated with such an idea.

If we take as axiomatic, then, that what we deem *critical* is a political construction, then we might inquire into which of those constructions are privileged. We have seen that the term *critical* has been appropriated by those who judge society and who do so with obvious Marxist leanings. This judging of society is for the purposes of exposing hidden power arrangements, oppressive practices, and ways of thinking. And it is also for the purpose of changing society to make it more just. This appropriation of the term can be traced to the work of critical theorists, especially those coming out of the Frankfurt school. The scholars and researchers affiliated with the Institute for Social Research, founded in 1923 in Frankfurt, Germany, attempted to revise both the Marxian critique of capitalism and the theory of revolution in order to confront those new social and political conditions that had evolved since Marx's death. In the process a "critical theory" of society emerged to deal with those aspects of social reality that Marx and his orthodox followers neglected or downplayed (Bronner and Kellner, 1989). These theorists were concerned with the social forces that moved and might be moved toward just institutions, but they were aware of the obstacles to radical change and sought to analyze and expose those obstacles. The critical theorists were concerned both with the interpretation of society and its transformation (Held, 1980).

Whether or not quantitative researchers want to pursue critique in similar fashion, critical theory does offer for those researchers—nay, any researcher in education—an important conceptual framework in two ways. First, critical theory, according to Bronner and Kellner (1989), offers a multidisciplinary approach to the study of society that combines perspectives drawn from political economy, sociology, cultural theory, philosophy, anthropology, and history. Such a multidisciplinary focus should be maintained by educational researchers not only because it provides a deeper analysis of societal problems but also because it draws attention away from the simplistic methodological debates that characterize much of the critique of educational research. Second, critical theory is unabashedly political. That is, unlike noncritical quantitative, and even many qualitative views, critical theory is sustained by an interest in emancipation from all forms of oppression, as well as by a commitment to freedom, happiness, and a rational ordering of society. Although we may disagree on what these ideas mean, the premise of critical theory—that its purpose is to transform society—is worth heeding when we seek to offer critique via quantitative data.

Therefore, we do not want to give up on the term *critical* as appropriated by those pursuing judgments of society, because that gives all researchers a political, and perhaps even moral, basis for coming together as critics. But we should resist the more recent attempts at capturing the term within methodological lines. For instance, we have seen a more recent appropriation of the term *critical*—still to offer judgments of society, *but only via philosophical, narrative, historical, anthropological, and other interpretive analyses*. This would exclude quantitative approaches to the judgment of society. Yet, the idea of *critical* has to remain open to different ways of pursing the ends at stake—the judgment of society and its most significant institutions, like higher education. Thus, some of what Kincheloe and McLaren (1994) assert is the agenda for critical qualitative research also seems like an appropriate agenda for critical quantitative research. They propose that "criticalist" researchers must attempt to use their work as a form of social or cultural criticism, and they must accept certain basic assumptions about society, assumptions that would exclude *positivist* research from what should appropriately be called critical but not quantitative research per se. These basic assumptions include the following: (1) all thought is fundamentally mediated by power relations that are socially and historically constituted; (2) facts can never be isolated from the domain of values or removed from some form of ideological inscription; (3) the relationship between concepts and objects is never stable or fixed and is often mediated by the social relations of capitalist production and consumption; (4) language is central to the formation of subjectivity; (5) certain groups in any society are privileged over others, and although the reasons for this privileging may vary widely, the oppression that characterizes contemporary societies is most forcefully reproduced when subordinates accept their social status as natural, necessary, or inevitable; (6) oppression has many faces and focusing on only one at the expense of others often elides the interconnections among them; and (7) mainstream research practices are generally, although most often unwittingly, implicated in the reproduction of systems of class, race, and gender oppression.

This latter assumption—that research is implicated in oppression—is worth fleshing out a bit more. There are ethical responsibilities associated with the critique of society. As critics *of* society, researchers must also be critical of their role *in* society. That is, critical researchers must be attentive to the privilege and authority that such a role carries, and to its potential to exert its own kind of oppression. Certainly, research that allows individuals to combat oppression, injustice, and inequality is well and good, but as Ellsworth (1989) argues about critical theories in education, we must keep in mind that what we offer as critical researchers is also a political program, a political agenda. And as such it must be subject to justification and to a questioning about its own use and support of authoritarian institutions (like colleges and universities, which favor some over others) and to the oppres-

NEW DIRECTIONS FOR INSTITUTIONAL RESEARCH • DOI: 10.1002/ir

sion that can take place when any political agenda is asserted as being "just," "good," "natural," "obvious," and so forth. Striving for social justice is a political goal, and so must be the research that allows us to pursue that goal. We must be attentive to how we unwittingly authorize some to speak and ensure the silence of others. For example, we must be leery of uncritically supporting research that advances efforts to open up selective institutions to previously excluded groups but does not also criticize the legitimacy of those institutions to dictate the course of our lives by being selective. Research that purports to be critical must actually be critical and self-critical. Indeed, given their importance in shaping the course of our lives, all researchers and scholars must be self-critical.

Gramsci's concept of the "organic intellectual" is useful here for rethinking the responsibility of the critical researcher and scholar. Gramsci (1971) proposes that organic intellectuals—as opposed to traditional intellectuals, who erroneously put themselves forward as autonomous and independent from class struggles—help organize a particular social group toward achieving its own ends and interests. To be truly revolutionary, to be truly critical of society, and to offer just alternatives, organic intellectuals must constantly defer personal gain and define themselves by the interests of their groups while not forgetting to remain critical of the group. The purpose of organic intellectuals is to question the commonsense notions that structure our lives and provide critical analyses of social problems. For critical researchers, this means not merely offering a critique of unjust social arrangements but also critical reflection on their own practices. Their critique, which is a judgment of society, is like all judgments in that it is inherently interpretive; what needs to be uncovered are the rules, often silent, that give value to some interpretations over others.

Having said before that I had thought methodology debates were irrelevant, I now realize that they are not so at all—not because I think there is anything particularly meaningful about any method in itself but because the overriding concern with methods prevents us from realizing how educational research offers the possibility of being critical and transformative. What we want to call critical research is a judgment of society for the purposes of changing it. This is how we can judge such critique: To what extent does research—any research—question society, to what extent does it offer suggestions for transforming society, and to what extent does it judge itself? This seems a good appropriation of the term *critical* for our purposes, and one that quantitative researchers should assert for themselves.

Thus, whether researchers can use quantitative data to answer critical questions is beside the point. The point is this: How do those researchers allow us to reflect on our society, how do they ask us to judge it, how do they propose we change it? Kincheloe and McLaren (1994) argue that inquiry that aspires to the name *critical* must be connected to an attempt to confront the injustice of a particular society or sphere within that society. Although traditional researchers cling to the guardrail of neutrality, they suggest, critical researchers frequently announce their partisanship in the struggle for a better world. This seems correct to me. So, although quantitative research is not often thought of as furthering these goals, there is absolutely no reason why it should not be thought of in such a way. Indeed, one must ask why any research can be said to be otherwise. Why are any researchers relieved of responsibility for the social world that they help create?

I ask the readers of this volume to ask themselves to what extent the researchers purporting to explain how quantitative data can answer critical questions actually expose the power of institutional arrangements that dictate how we live and work, especially in colleges and universities. These researchers use quantitative data, but do they critique those institutional arrangements by using that quantitative data? These studies should not be judged for the accuracy of the social realities they espouse (or assume) or for the rigor of the methods they use, but for the questions they ask and the critiques they offer. Talburt (2002) suggests that we think about research not for its veracity but for how it opens up new lines of thought. I agree with this. We must let go of the idea of the all-knowing researcher, which ultimately forces us to focus on methods, and allow ourselves the freedom to ask questions and to engage with others in a discussion that presents the possibility of seeing our world differently. The world can be transformed only when it is seen differently than it was before. It is in this way that critical research is the most practical thing we can offer to higher education. The point of research is not simply to interpret the world but, following Marx, to change it.

References

Altbach, P. G. "Research, Policy, and Administration in Higher Education." *Review of Higher Education,* 1998, *21,* 205–207.

Barone, T. "Science, Art, and the Predispositions of Educational Researchers." *Educational Researcher,* 2001, 24(7), 25–28.

Bronner, S. E., and Kellner, D. M. (eds.). *Critical Theory and Society: A Reader.* New York: Routledge, 1989.

Conrad, C. F. "Meditations on the Ideology of Inquiry in Higher Education: Exposition, Critique, and Conjecture." *Review of Higher Education,* 1989, *12,* 199–220.

Constas, M. A. "The Changing Nature of Educational Research and a Critique of Postmodernism." *Educational Researcher,* 1998a, 27(2), 26–33.

Constas, M. A. "Deciphering Postmodern Educational Research." *Educational Researcher,* 1998b, 27(9), 36–42.

Creswell, J. W., Goodchild, L. F., and Turner, P. P. "Integrated Qualitative and Quantitative Research: Epistemology, History, and Designs." In J. Smart (ed.), *Higher Education: Handbook of Theory and Research,* Vol. 11 (pp. 90–136). New York: Agathon Press, 1996.

Eisner, W. W. "The Promise and Perils of Alternative Forms of Data Representation." *Educational Researcher,* 1997, 26(6), 4–10.

Ellsworth, E. "Why Doesn't This Feel Empowering? Working Through the Repressive Myths of Critical Pedagogy." *Harvard Educational Review,* 1989, *59,* 297–324.

Gramsci, A. *Selections from the Prison Notebooks of Antonio Gramsci.* (Q. Hoare, ed.; G. N. Smith, trans.). New York: International Publishers, 1971.

Guba, E. G., and Lincoln, Y. S. "Competing Paradigms in Qualitative Research." In N. K. Denzin and Y. S. Lincoln (eds.), *Handbook of Qualitative Research* (pp. 105–117). Thousand Oaks, Calif.: Sage, 1994.

Held, D. *Introduction to Critical Theory: Horkheimer to Habermas.* Berkeley: University of California Press, 1980.

Keller, G. "Does Higher Education Research Need Revisions?" *Review of Higher Education,* 1998, *21,* 267–278.

Kincheloe, J. L., and McLaren, P. L. "Rethinking Critical Theory and Qualitative Research." In N. K. Denzin and Y. S. Lincoln (eds.), *Handbook of Qualitative Research* (pp. 138–157). Thousand Oaks, Calif.: Sage, 1994.

Mayer, R. E. "What Is the Place of Science in Educational Research?" *Educational Researcher,* 2000, *29*(6), 38–39.

Mayer, R. E. "Resisting the Assault on Science: The Case for Evidence-Based Reasoning in Educational Research." *Educational Researcher,* 2001, *30*(7), 29–30.

Oxford English Dictionary. Oxford: Oxford University Press, 1989.

Schwandt, T. A. "Constructivist, Interpretivist Approaches to Human Inquiry." In N. K. Denzin and Y. S. Lincoln (eds.), *Handbook of Qualitative Research* (pp. 118–137). Thousand Oaks, Calif.: Sage, 1994.

Talburt, S. "Verify Data." Paper presented at the annual meeting of the Association for the Study of Higher Education, Sacramento, Nov. 2002.

Tierney, W. G. "On Translation: From Research Findings to Public Utility." *Theory into Practice,* 2000, *39,* 185–190.

Williams, R. *Keywords: A Vocabulary of Culture and Society.* (Rev. ed.) Oxford: Oxford University Press, 1983.

Willinsky, J. "The Strategic Education Research Program and the Public Value of Research." *Educational Researcher,* 2001, *30*(1), 5–14.

Wolcott, H. F. "Ethnographic Research in Education." In R. M. Jaeger (ed.), *Complementary Methods for Research in Education* (2nd ed.; pp. 327–353). Washington, D.C.: American Educational Research Association, 1988.

BENJAMIN BAEZ is associate professor of higher education in the Department of Educational Leadership and Policy Studies at Florida International University.

3

This chapter serves as a guide for quantitative researchers who seek to approach their research questions critically.

Bridging Key Research Dilemmas: Quantitative Research Using a Critical Eye

Deborah Faye Carter, Sylvia Hurtado

For many of us who use quantitative methodology on a regular basis, we confront constraints while at the same time attempting to stretch the boundaries of current theory and develop models relevant to specific populations. This becomes clearer over the course of a long-term research agenda, because the topics we choose and who we are as researchers become evident through our work. In this chapter, we explore several key research dilemmas and potential solutions for quantitative researchers intent on using a critical eye for examining current theory and models.

These dilemmas involve describing how the role of the quantitative researcher becomes apparent on examination of a body of work, the choice between comparing groups or highlighting variability in a single group, choosing approaches for generalizability or context specificity, and remaining "distant" or participating in action research. Finally, we propose potential solutions to some of these dilemmas, which we have confronted in our own work.

In this chapter, we argue that (1) quantitative research is not wholly objective and that there are ways in which autobiography can intersect with research; (2) critical quantitative approaches identify discrepancies between theory and fact; and (3) there are positives and negatives for comparative group versus context-specific approaches to understanding group differences.

New Directions for Institutional Research, no. 133, Spring 2007 © Wiley Periodicals, Inc.
Published online in Wiley InterScience (www.interscience.wiley.com) • DOI: 10.1002/ir.202

25

Finding the Intersection Between Autobiography and Research

First, we insist there is an intersection of autobiography and research for quantitative researchers. Why is there no room for exploring the role of quantitative researchers in their work as there is in qualitative work? One of the main reasons for this absence is the age-old assumption that remaining an "objective" and distant researcher is preferable and lends confidence to the work. However, a great deal of quantitative research that claims to be objective really is politically motivated and perhaps biased regarding issues of race in higher education (Rothman, Lipset, and Nevitte, 2003). We would do well to know the autobiographies of quantitative researchers to judge more astutely the work at two levels: the extent to which the work is a rigorous test of a theory or hypothesis and achieves its objective and how this fits into the overall work of these researchers in their long-term goals to improve education or shift its purpose. In this chapter, we devote attention to the first level, although it may escape the scrutiny of peer review on occasion. The second level is rarely discussed or explored in formal settings.

As women of color, it is evident in our work that our main goal is to improve higher education for the success of diverse college students in a variety of contexts. In many ways, we study the underrepresented populations in higher education because of our own unique experiences in higher education. We attempt to unpack our own college experience examining hundreds and sometimes thousands of students from backgrounds not unlike our own because we understand there is something unique about that experience (and overcoming the odds of failure) that deserves explanation. We seek to educate others and test our own intuitive hypotheses about the way the world works. It drives us to develop better questions, more relevant models for diverse student populations, and to understand whether the issues of this generation of students are the same as for our own generation. With every test of a model using a distinct population, we attempt to break down the theory, document alternative experiences, and begin to construct new models (Hurtado and Carter, 1997). This cannot and should not be the work of only qualitative methodologists.

Another reason exists to explore the intersection of autobiography and research, and that is that the role of objectivity is being questioned at all levels in methodology (Harding, 1991). Krathwohl (1998) describes new ways to determine the distinction between a researcher's observations and how others may view the same phenomenon. These distinctions have yet to find their way into quantitative methods. Furthermore, quantitative methods cannot remain unchanged by recent questions raised in science, feminist studies, and advancements in qualitative methodology. For example, critical theories and qualitative approaches question the notion of objectivity, how best to represent multiple perspectives, and how the researcher is involved in the design and interpretation of findings.

NEW DIRECTIONS FOR INSTITUTIONAL RESEARCH • DOI: 10.1002/ir

We acknowledge, however, that there are strong pressures fo sus about research approach and how one employs the scientific n educational research, which come essentially from a field that is in of struggle about whether or not there is a predominant paradigm. In the *Structure of Scientific Revolutions,* Kuhn (1996) states that paradigm-based research is "an attempt to force nature into the preformed and relatively inflexible box" (p. 24). When researchers in a field attempt to establish consensus about a prevailing paradigm, there is little effort to call forth new sets of phenomena. Further, there are few attempts to discover anomalies, and when they do emerge, they are discarded or overlooked. For example, how many times have we ignored the fact that our models typically are less likely to explain one group's behavior when compared with another (for example, examining the variance explained in educational outcomes for black females when compared with white females or men)?

Moreover, "normal scientific research is directed to the articulation of those phenomena and theories that the paradigm already supplies" (Kuhn, 1996, p. 24). This suggests that the challenge is simply in figuring how to solve a puzzle for an answer that we are almost sure already exists. It also suggests very little interest in new theory development, or modification of existing theories, and presupposes that we already know the theories to test. The focus then becomes confirmation and replication and not on generating new models or ways of thinking about the important issues and relevance to the improvement of practice. This is a central dilemma, particularly now that the U.S. Department of Education has attempted over the last few years to push experimental research as the predominant and "valid" research approach in education. It provides evidence of pressure to restrict the researcher's vision, apply rigid rules of science, resist varied forms of epistemology, and neglect dynamic conditions in the field of practice. In important areas of practice that involve inequity in education and achievement, it may not yet be possible to improve the educational problems we observe within the confines of what is known or within the frames of current theory. New discoveries are necessary and are only possible by training researchers to maintain a critical eye for new phenomena.

Identifying Discrepancies Between Theory and Fact

Kuhn (1996) suggests that we can employ normal science and advance discovery by paying attention to discrepancies between theory and fact. That is, we can come up with a series of facts that no longer fit our theories and begin to call into question the existing theory, urge its modification, or encourage new theory building. We can do so when adopting new models and measures that might help explain the experiences of particular groups, especially those whose educational experiences and achievement we are interested in improving. This was the approach we took in attempting to understand Latino students' sense of belonging in college (Hurtado and Carter, 1997).

In that study, we sought to test conceptually how Latino students experience integration into the college community. Tinto's 1993 theory makes a distinction between student participation in academic and social systems in colleges and universities and academic and social "integration." Further, we argued that the notion of integration may be distinct still from students of color who are entering predominantly white college environments.

The core issues we explored were the distinction between students' psychological sense of their membership in the campus community and their actual participation in campus life. With respect to students' actual participation in campus life, we posited that students of color attending predominantly white institutions must interact in multiple worlds (that of their own cultural group and that of other cultural groups) and therefore often have multiple memberships in campus communities.

As a result of our study, we advocated departures from Tinto's model to allow for greater understanding of students' transitional dilemmas, how campus programs can help students adjust to the college experience, and how students' memberships in various communities contribute to the concept of cohesion or marginalization on campuses.

Quantitative researchers face other dilemmas that can also be decided to help devote greater attention to anomalous phenomena that may lead to advancements of practice and our understanding of educational issues. These include determining when to use a comparative group versus a group-specific approach to a research issue, choosing an approach to highlight generalizability of findings or to highlight the findings specific to a particular context, and determining when to conduct research "objectively" distanced or to participate in action research. In addition, the uses of new theory can lead to new ways of looking at an issue that have remained unexplained or examined in previous work. The advantages and disadvantages of each approach are explained and, finally, ways to resolve such dilemmas are highlighted at the end of the chapter.

Using a Comparative Group Approach Versus a Group-Specific Focus. A typical mechanism for examining group differences is to use dichotomous variables in a regression model or an analysis of variance (ANOVA) to determine differences. One advantage to developing a single statistical model and using dichotomous variables to examine group differences or ANOVA is that a single model may apply to various groups of students. For research studies that have smaller sample sizes, the study may not have appropriate statistical power if separate group analyses are performed.

There are some limitations to using single statistical models to examine group differences. Although using dichotomous variables can account for some differences, in statistical models where several variables differ across racial and ethnic groups, a single statistical model can eclipse the circumstances under which some variables may differ across groups. It is true that interaction terms can help tease out specific effects, but what if there are many independent variables in the model? This requires a hypothesis or rationale for each interaction term. We believe it is not practical to construct dozens of interaction terms and that a comparative group approach may be needed instead in order to conduct a more complex investigation of group differences.

Comparative Group Approach. The comparative group approach refers to the method of conducting statistical analyses separately by group. There has been research that suggests that minority groups experience achievement processes in a different manner than white students. The comparative group approach would involve examining achievement processes separately by racial or ethnic group. This is an appropriate technique if the researcher already knows (based on previous research) that there are likely to be group differences and that something useful can be gleaned from completing the analyses separately. The benefit of separate group analyses is that variables that affect groups differently can be clearly seen. Some variables may have strong positive effects for one group but no significant effect or a negative effect for another group.

Another benefit of comparative group analysis is that it can provide a context for understanding findings. For instance, St. John (1991) found that African Americans are less likely to attend college than White students, but that after taking into account degree aspirations, African American students are as likely (or perhaps more likely) to attend college. This indicates that there are important social and contextual variables that can be eclipsed if comparative analyses are not performed or groups of students are analyzed together.

A limitation of separate group analyses is that it may be difficult to compare groups if the sample sizes are uneven. Some adjustment to statistical coefficients may need to be made to make valid comparisons. Also, in the need to construct comparable statistical models across groups, the individual groups may not receive enough attention. For instance, there may be some factors affecting certain student groups that have little relevance for the compared groups—but these factors need to be included in all comparative group models so useful comparisons can be made. For instance, "Language Spoken at Home" could yield different results for African American populations than for Asian American or Latino groups. Comparing results on that measure across groups will necessitate explanation and interpretations that are specific to certain groups.

Specific Group Approach. Another approach is to focus research on a specific group. For instance, a researcher may decide to study only the Latino population. A strength of this approach in quantitative research is that more of the group's internal variability can be examined. A researcher could intentionally sample various ethnicities in that population (for example, Puerto Rican, Mexican, Brazilian, Cuban, El Salvadoran, and so on) to study how they differ. Using this research approach, researchers may be able to employ more complex analyses to understand within-group heterogeneity as well as how such issues as generation status and language spoken at home uniquely affect the different ethnic groups.

Choosing an Approach for Generalizability or for Context Specificity. In judging quantitative research, one of the key considerations is its generalizability. In designing a study, we often pay attention to careful selection of types of institutions and of student populations in those institutions to ensure both representation and generalizability. We have more confidence in findings that may hold true across a number of contexts and that represent some standard of universal truth. It is the preferred research standard. If it is not generalizable, we expect the quantitative researcher to state the limitations of the study and explain how these findings may not be applicable to all students in all higher education settings. It is important to note that, on average, the generalizable findings will hold for all students and institutions; however, researchers are less likely to emphasize how the findings might be variable. Instead, we simply encourage others to replicate the work to confirm its generalizability across contexts and populations. Educational research has recently come under criticism for far fewer replication studies than in other fields (Berliner, 2002), so it may be less likely that our findings will be confirmed in a reasonable time frame. In short, we need to recognize that the issue of generalizability remains an important but rather elusive goal in practice.

Researchers not only neglect to mention when their studies may fail to apply to students outside of "the average" but tend to view such departures as anomalies. We contend that perhaps the most interesting part of a study may indeed be these departures. They require closer examination and insist on a more critical eye. Departures from average norms suggest habits or experiences of students that cannot conform to "one-size-fits-all" higher education settings and practices. Taking note of these departures may be critical to improving practice.

This leads us to another consideration in choosing a research approach to address generalizability—that is, it may be more difficult to adapt an "average finding" to practices that are typically contextual. There can be a gap between what the research says works and what really works in practice (we return to this issue in a subsequent section). It is even more dangerous to assume that findings in one context or study are applicable in another context—the true test of generalizability must provide evidence that a finding is indeed applicable in other contexts and student populations. For example, increasing students' social integration to improve student retention is not as possible at a community college as it is at a four-year residential college; one reason is that working students do not rely on college for social activities. Yet the assumption is that social integration is such a universal proposition that it must be enacted at all institutions. Much more research is needed on the specific context to determine the unique institutional and experiential elements of student retention for community college students—and it is highly likely the answer lies inside rather than outside the classroom.

Generalizability must be linked back to context if we seek to improve education, and this provides some support for conducting context-specific studies without apologies for lack of generalizability. In fact, a context-specific study can be rationalized that it contributes to understanding generalizability because there is some doubt about the universality of published findings until proven applicable in a variety of contexts. Context-specific studies can then be used to question widely accepted models and findings that inform practice, provide insight into departures from theses theories and research findings, and begin to suggest unique models. The context-specific approach also allows for stronger links with actual practices in institutions. Here is where institutional research is important in the grand scheme of educational research: it can be informed by prevailing theories and research but also more finely attuned to the need to improve practices in specific institutional contexts. It is decidedly context-specific and plays an important role in understanding the universality of truths we uncover in our efforts to improve postsecondary education.

There are some important cautions to consider in a context-specific approach. First, some models are developed for single institutions and these may be too unique to adapt to other contexts. We need to require researchers to highlight these unique aspects of the context in which their study is conducted. This allows others to judge whether a similar study or its findings are applicable to other contexts. For many researchers not engaged in institutional research, where there exists a great deal of familiarity with the context, a context-specific approach requires more field-intensive work to grapple with the unique culture and climate and student body at the institution. This information needs to be shared with readers of the published research.

Second, context-specific studies still need to adhere to methodological rigor, even if the setting focuses on a specific group or groups or environment. Braxton, McKinney, and Reynolds (2006) surveyed the retention data from a few dozen colleges and universities and concluded that most of the studies did not employ sufficient methodological rigor—either in terms of using appropriate multivariate statistical tests or the use and application of theory. Important quantitative work can be done with a critical eye, and such work needs to remain methodologically sound.

Conducting Research Objectively or Participating in Action Research. Many of the quantitative educational research traditions are based on the scientific method. These traditions (which are also referred to as *postpositivist*) focus on examining "causes that influence outcomes" (Creswell, 2002, p. 7). Most quantitative research begins with testing a particular theory even if a postpositive perspective acknowledges that there is no absolute truth and that no research study or research methods are perfect. However, postpositive frameworks still assume objectivity in the research and most researchers "must examine their methods and conclusions for bias" (p. 8).

Although a core assumption of the scientific method and postpositivism is that of objective orientation, this assumption may not be accurate. Researchers have particular assumptions and biases that can affect the kinds of measures used, the data collected, the participants involved in the research, the statistical methods used, and the interpretations of the results. Two theoretical approaches that are often associated with qualitative research can be applied to quantitative approaches as well: critical race theory and action research.

Critical theories—theories that critically examine social roles and institutions—are gaining recognition in higher education research. One example of a critical theory is critical race theory (CRT).

> Critical [race] theory is a framework or set of basic insights, perspectives, methods, and pedagogy that seeks to identify, analyze, and transform those structural and cultural aspects of higher education that maintain the marginal position and subordination of [people of color]. . . . Critical race theory suggests that while those on the social margins have less access to opportunities and resources, they also experience different barriers, obstacles, or other forms of individual and societal oppression than those at the center. (Solórzano and Villalpando, 1998, pp. 212–214)

Many researchers have used CRT frameworks for qualitative methods (see Solórzano, 2001, for one example), but the philosophical framework can be applied to quantitative research as well. It is possible to examine phenomena with objectivity and weigh alternative explanations where appropriate while also advocating for social justice and for the reduction of racism.

Action research—like critical race theory—advocates for the researcher becoming immersed in the research and using that research to inform changes in practice (McNiff, 2002). A key element of action research is the feedback between the researcher-practitioner and the system being researched. Once phenomena are identified and studied, recommendations for changes in practice are developed and the effect of these changes can then be studied. All of this forms a constant loop of activity in which the researcher-practitioner can be constantly engaged. Research as a catalyst for change or a form of advocacy is not a new approach, but this approach can be an effective means for conducting quantitative research on marginalized groups and for populations where simultaneous interventions and research are needed.

New Directions for Quantitative Research

How have we begun to bridge these research dilemmas? Although we have provided some directives in our explanation of these dilemmas, here we summarize potential solutions that are derived from our own work. First, although we insist there is an intersection of autobiography and research for users of quantitative methodology, our field is far from accepting the notion that we should lay bare the biases we bring into the research process even as it has become more standard practice for qualitative researchers who serve as the "instruments" of data collection, analysis, and interpretation. There is still the notion that we should be free of politics to engage in the search for truth, and we wish to preserve such autonomy. However, at the same time, education (its funding, administration, and implicit assumptions that underlie practice) is not entirely free of politics and it would be a mistake to think our research occurs independently of these political debates or our own frames of reference that come from our educational, professional, and social backgrounds.

We do encourage all researchers to begin to share this information, just as we have attempted to share here our long-range goals and hopes for educational improvement. We can begin to explain more about the intent, motivations, and objectives of our approach and to take responsibility for the aims we wish to achieve (such as improving educational opportunity for students of color) without compromising rigor, replicability, and responsibility. The role of the researcher is important, but should not be privileged or overemphasized at the expense of the important research questions that merit careful and rigorous examination. We are also frank in acknowledging that some of our audiences, intent on finding answers or information, such as the users of institutional research, simply do not care to know the researcher. So the solution involves knowing one's audience and finding a place to insert the role of quantitative researcher where appropriate. For those of us with professional higher education experiences, it can even lend credence to research in its link with practice.

If we see each research dilemma presented here as an either-or decision or proposition, a viable solution is not possible. It is important to acknowledge flexibility in research design to allow something in between for wider use of our findings. For example, if most studies select either a comparative group approach or group-specific approach, there is still room for a solution that bridges these approaches in creating a new design. One such design may use a comparative study to focus a group-specific approach. This involves conducting analysis on the entire population and on a specific population of interest as well, to determine whether unique models are required, and then providing further explanation about these departures. For studies lacking the same data on a more general population, another solution is to provide an adequate review of research that has generated "normative" findings as a backdrop for exploring how a specific population conforms or departs substantially from traditional models or research focused on more general populations (Hurtado and Carter, 1997).

These solutions parallel another approach that can be used to address generalizability and context specificity. For example, for many years the Cooperative Institutional Research Program (CIRP) has encouraged institutions to use its surveys to examine their own environments and compare themselves to national, normative data or peer institutions (Higher Education Research Institute, 2005). This is extremely useful for institutional researchers, and the cooperative nature of the design allows for these helpful comparisons to decide if a student body at a particular campus is unique or much like the average across the nation. Further breakdowns of the data can determine if this is true for specific student populations as well. It addresses the needs of context-specific information and more universal principles of student behavior, values, skills, and attitudes. Consortia or collaborating institutions share data to discover what works across the campuses and what may work on their own particular campuses. More recently, general research on public universities provides a backdrop for the individual collaborating institutions to examine their own student experiences and models for improving undergraduate education (Hurtado, 2003). Meetings were held with members of all participating campuses to also share practices to achieve key undergraduate education goals.

Still another solution is to mix quantitative methodology (for providing an overview of issues and concerns) with qualitative methodology (for exploring contexts and specific populations in-depth) when knowledge about specific issues and concerns is lacking. Clearly quantitative methods are best suited when we can anticipate questions to ask and theory to test. However, we may still have difficulty interpreting results without information about context or student experiences. This is where qualitative research can be helpful to inform the findings. Using a mixed-method research design can help us achieve goals for generalizability and context specificity, allowing us to assume a more critical eye toward the limitations of what we can know for each technique.

The final dilemma on achieving distance as opposed to engaging in action research forces us to identify ways to convert research into improvements in practice. Action research is more often used in the case of interventions, corrections based on results, and revision of interventions. If we are not charged with implementation of intervention or its evaluation, we should find ways to partner with practitioners who will implement the research findings. At the very least, we should step out of our roles as distant researchers on occasion to encourage the use of research findings in improving practice. This involves putting our research into the hands of those who need the information, and evaluating our work by the impact it has on actual educational practice.

References

Berliner, D. C. "Educational Research: The Hardest Science of All." *Educational Researcher,* 2002, *31*(8), 18–20.

Braxton, J. M., McKinney, J. S., and Reynolds, P. "Cataloging Institutional Efforts to Understand and Reduce College Student Departure." In E. P. St. John and M. Wilkersons (eds.), *Reframing Persistence Research to Improve Academic Success.* New Directions for Institutional Research, no. 130. San Francisco: Jossey-Bass, 2006.

Creswell, J. W. *Research Design: Qualitative, Quantitative, and Mixed Methods Approaches.* Thousand Oaks, Calif.: Sage, 2002.

Harding, S. "Whose Science? Whose Knowledge? Thinking from Women's Lives." Ithaca, N.Y.: Cornell University Press, 1991.

Higher Education Research Institute. *The American Freshman: National Norms for 2004.* Los Angeles: University of California, 2005.

Hurtado, S. "Are We Achieving the Promise of Diversity?" *Liberal Education,* 2003, *88*(2), 12–13.

Hurtado, S., and Carter, D. F. "Effects of College Transition and Perceptions of the Campus Racial Climate on Latino College Students' Sense of Belonging." *Sociology of Education,* Oct. 1997, *70*, 324–345.

Krathwohl, D. R. *Methods of Educational and Social Science Research: An Integrated Approach.* (2nd ed.) Reading, Mass.: Addison-Wesley, 1998.

Kuhn, T. S. *The Structure of Scientific Revolutions.* (3rd ed.) Chicago: University of Chicago Press, 1996.

McNiff, J. *Action Research: Principles and Practice.* London: Routledge, 2002.

Rothman, S., Lipset, S. M., and Nevitte, N. "Racial Diversity Reconsidered." *Public Interest,* Spring 2003, *151*, 25–38.

Solórzano, D. G. "Critical Race Theory, Racial Microaggressions, and Campus Racial Climate: The Experiences of African American College Students." *Journal of Negro Education,* 2001, *69*(1), 60–73.

Solórzano, D. G., and Villalpando, O. "Critical Race Theory, Marginality, and the Experience of Students of Color in Higher Education." In C. A. Torres and T. R. Mitchell (eds.), *Sociology of Education: Emerging Perspectives.* Albany: State University of New York Press, 1998.

St. John, E. P. "What Really Influences Minority Attendance? Sequential Analyses of the High School and Beyond Sophomore Cohort." *Research in Higher Education,* 1991, *32*(2), 141–158.

Tinto, V. *Leaving College: Rethinking the Causes and Cures of Student Attrition.* (2nd ed.) Chicago: University of Chicago Press, 1993.

DEBORAH FAYE CARTER *is associate professor and director of the Center for the Study of Higher and Postsecondary Education at the University of Michigan.*

SYLVIA HURTADO *is professor in the Graduate School of Education and Information Studies and director of the Higher Education Research Institute at the University of California, Los Angeles.*

Cross-sectional frameworks, or between-group approaches, in quantitative research in higher education have limitations that hinder what we know about the intersection of race and educational opportunities and outcomes.

Race, Ethnicity, and Higher Education Policy: The Use of Critical Quantitative Research

Robert T. Teranishi

The uneven distribution of opportunities and disparate outcomes for students of different racial backgrounds has been a stubbornly persistent problem in U.S. higher education. In the world of education policy, however, Asian American students remain at the margins (Nakanishi, 1995; Teranishi, 2005a). There is a lack of reliable and informative policy research on Asian Americans, which is confounded by stubborn and persistent stereotypes and assumptions that are not grounded in empirical research (Teranishi, 2005b; Zia, 2006). Generalizations and falsehoods about this population operate as conceptual blockages that inhibit the inclusion and fair treatment of Asian Americans in policy considerations (Zia, 2006).

This chapter discusses how cross-sectional frameworks, or between-group approaches, in quantitative research in higher education have limitations that hinder what we know about the intersection of race and educational opportunities and outcomes generally, and the Asian American experience in higher education specifically. I use examples from my own research on the participation and representation of Asian American students in U.S. higher education to demonstrate that critical frameworks in quantitative research can yield important and interesting perspectives that can be applied to the study of other racial groups in order to improve what we know about subpopulations in broader racial categories. Specifically, I examine the utility of critical race theory to meeting these objectives. I argue that

New Directions for Institutional Research, no. 133, Spring 2007 © Wiley Periodicals, Inc.
Published online in Wiley InterScience (www.interscience.wiley.com) • DOI: 10.1002/ir.203

research designs that are commonly applied to the study of black, Latino, Native American, *and* Asian American students neither promote a better understanding about any individual racial population nor provide a perspective that allows us to constructively improve their educational experiences or outcomes.

Normative Approaches to Studying Race

The exclusion and misrepresentation of the Asian American population in educational research and policy is often attributed to limitations in data (Hune and Chan, 1997; Hune, 2002; Teranishi, 2005a). In fact, many national databases are not designed to accommodate distinctions within the Asian American population (Nakanishi, 1995; Teranishi, 2005a). Despite the lack of research and data available to conduct research, there are many assumptions about the relative success of the population. As a result, Asian Americans possess a paradoxical position as a *highly visible* and successful group in attaining higher education, yet *invisible* in education research and policy.

Other problems associated with the study of Asian Americans can be traced to the conceptualization of research that positions Asian Americans inside a black-white racial framework (Chang, 1999; Kim, 1999; Teranishi, 2003). In this framework, the experiences, outcomes, and representation of Asian Americans are examined vis-à-vis blacks and whites, with Asian Americans in the middle often serving as the "wildcard" to support or dispute an argument about another racial group (Takagi, 1992). This was notable in the recent book by William Bowen, Martin Kurzweil, and Eugene Tobin, *Equity and Excellence in American Higher Education* (2005). Like many other important books in the debate on access and equity in higher education, this book labeled blacks and Latinos as "minorities" whereas Asian Americans and Pacific Islanders (AAPIs) were considered "non-minorities" along with their white counterparts. AAPIs are simply selectively included in analysis that helps make a point of the relative disadvantage of "minority" groups.

The lack of research on and assumptions about different racial minority populations can be traced to the research paradigms that are often applied to the study of race in higher education. The most common approach to comparative racial analysis is often driven by a normative racial framework. Normative frameworks are designed to identify populations that may warrant resources or services that can help close the gap identified in the research—essentially, the goal is to identify how different racial groups are unevenly distributed across a particular outcome (that is, participation, graduation, GPA, and so on).

In many cases, studies are not designed to critically examine, acknowledge, or appreciate the heterogeneity that exists in a racial group. Rather, comparative racial frameworks assume that racial categories as a whole are consistently homogeneous across groups with regard to their characteristics. As a result, the actual educational experiences and processes of students from different racial groups as a whole, and as distinct parts, are often concealed. By adopting a comparative racial framework that combines broad racial groups, we assume that there is enough consistency in the homogeneity within racial groups that they are equally comparable and the instruments used to measure differences across groups are universally applicable. I argue that racial groups are neither equally nor consistently comparable and that the approaches to studying differing student populations are not universally applicable. Critical race theory (CRT) has been identified as an effective lens for identifying and addressing policy gaps for racial minorities by bringing race to the fore, breaking down assumptions about racial groups, and being critical of systems and policies (Solórzano, 1998). This chapter applies tenants of CRT to identify and examine key policy issues that affect the population.

Critical Race Theory and Quantitative Research

Critical race theory is used in higher education research to help understand the educational experiences of students of color by centering the dialogue on the issue of race as the core of the discussion (Delgado, 1995; Solórzano, Villalpando, and Oseguera, 2005). Solórzano (1998) explains that "critical race theory in education challenges the traditional claims of the educational system and its institutions to objectivity, meritocracy, color and gender blindness, race and gender neutrality, and equal opportunity" (p. 122). Thus, an understanding of the educational experiences of the Asian American and Pacific Islander population requires a framework that acknowledges the unique racialized status of Asian Americans, as well as their social, political, and structural positions in society.

Conceptually, critical race theory in education challenges ahistoricism and the unidisciplinary focus of most analyses and centralizes race and racism in education by placing them in both an historical and contemporary context using interdisciplinary methods (Delgado, 1995, 1989; Garcia, 1995; Harris, 1994; Olivas, 1990). CRT challenges the dominant discourse on race and racism in education by examining how educational theory, policy, and practice have been used to subordinate certain racial and ethnic groups (Solórzano, 1998).

I use CRT as a lens to problematize traditional notions of race by examining the intersections of ethnicity, social class, and immigration among the Asian American population (Bell, 1987; Carrasco, 1996; Delgado, 1989, 1995; Olivas, 1990). These characteristics of the Asian American population have often been masked by research paradigms that place this population in a black-white racial framework. The consequences of this approach results in the study of Asian Americans determined by the frameworks to understand inequities of African Americans vis-à-vis whites. From this perspective, blacks and Latinos are viewed predominantly as inferior, underprivileged, or underrepresented, and as underachievers. Conversely, resilient and successful students are considered "models" (Stanton-Salazar and Spina, 2001). Allen (1999) cites this paradigm as commonly applied to educational research as a "misguided and counterproductive game of 'oppression sweepstakes'" (pp. 206–207), whereby various groups are pitted against one another in competition for the dubious status of "Year's Most Oppressed." Rather, there is a tremendous need to acknowledge the diverse experiences that exist among marginalized populations, including Asian Americans.

Critical race theory has also been found to be an innovative interpretive framework for researchers, policymakers, and practitioners to challenge mainstream approaches to higher education policy analysis (Solórzano and Villalpando, 1998; Solórzano, Villalpando, and Oseguera, 2005; Tate, 1997). CRT asserts that the needs of marginalized populations, as opposed to the agenda served by normative frameworks, are often overlooked. Therefore, CRT is an effective lens for examining and challenging normative paradigms, which define mainstream policy problems and determine appropriate concerns for research in education. Moreover, CRT can be used as a way not only to understand policies and decision making and their impact on a population but also to look critically at the very presumptions and reasoning that underlie them. These presumptions often go unquestioned and unchallenged.

Critical Race Theory and the Asian American Educational Experience

Important trends exist in the distribution of Asian Americans in U.S. higher education that are masked by comparative racial frameworks. Key assumptions have driven the treatment of AAPIs in policy and research. With regard to the distribution of Asian Americans in U.S. higher education, they are often presented as overrepresented in U.S. higher education, concentrated *only* in selective four-year universities, or a "successful" minority group with no academic challenges. Here these assumptions are examined through the analytic lens of critical race theory. The analysis concludes with implications for policy and research.

Asian American Participation in U.S. Higher Education. AAPI participation in U.S. higher education can be traced back to the midnineteenth century. However, their sizeable presence in higher education, which coincides with the growth in their population overall following the 1965 Immigration Act, mainly occurred after 1970. Between 1980 and 1990, the AAPI student population doubled, and it nearly tripled between 1980 and 2000 (Teranishi, 2005a). Although this growth is impressive, this participation is misleading because there is a large concentration of Asian Americans in a small number of institutions. Two-thirds of all Asian American college students nationally are concentrated in two hundred institutions out of over four thousand Title IV institutions in the United States (Teranishi, 2005a). These two hundred institutions represent less than 5 percent of all Title IV institutions. Three-quarters of all Asian

American college students nationally are concentrated in fewer than three hundred institutions in the United States. The distribution of Asian Americans across a small number of institutions is nearly always overlooked in research and policy considerations.

Asian American enrollment is also highly concentrated in a small number of states. In 2000, nearly two-thirds of all Asian American college students attended college in eight states. Nearly half of all Asian American college students nationally attended college in California, New York, and Texas. The distribution of Asian American college students in 2000 was actually much wider than in past decades. In 1980, two-thirds of all Asian American college students attended college in four states.

Although there is tremendous growth in Asian American college participation, the distribution and representation should be disaggregated by institutional type. Higher education in the United States is highly stratified by control (public versus private), selectivity (selective versus nonselective), and degree type (two-year versus four-year). Despite the assumption that Asian Americans are only concentrated in selective four-year institutions, there is evidence to the contrary. When total enrollment is disaggregated by institutional type, the sizeable concentration of Asian Americans in community colleges is apparent. In 2000, there was a larger proportion of Asian American students attending public two-year institutions (44.4 percent) in the United States than four-year public institutions (43.2 percent) (Teranishi, 2005a).

Finally, it is not uncommon for studies on race in higher education to completely leave out Asian Americans from the analysis. Alternatively, there is another trend where Asian Americans are included as "others" along with Native Americans and other students who do not fall into a black, white, or Latino category. As a result, very little is known about the Asian American educational experience, including their participation, satisfaction, and outcomes in U.S. higher education.

Misrepresentation. Often, because of a lack of careful and critical approaches to the study of race in higher education, we make generalizations about Asian Americans that are inaccurate and misleading. For example, whereas data from the *Eighth Annual Status Report on Minorities in Higher Education* (Carter and Wilson, 1989) show that in 1998 32 percent of doctorates conferred in the United States were to "Asians," 86 percent of these degrees were actually conferred to international students from Asia, rather than "Asian Americans" (see Figure 4.1). A recent NSF publication reported that in the time period, doctoral degrees awarded to Asians who were U.S. citizens accounted for a mere 2 percent of all doctoral degrees awarded (Thurgood, Golloday, and Hill, 2006).

By reporting these racial categories and including international students, we use inflated numbers that exaggerate the achievement of Asian Americans. Such inflations prompt some scholars to describe Asian Americans as overrepresented in terms of earned doctorates; they are actually underrepresented.

NEW DIRECTIONS FOR INSTITUTIONAL RESEARCH • DOI: 10.1002/ir

Figure 4.1. Doctorates Conferred, by Race and U.S. Citizenship, 1998

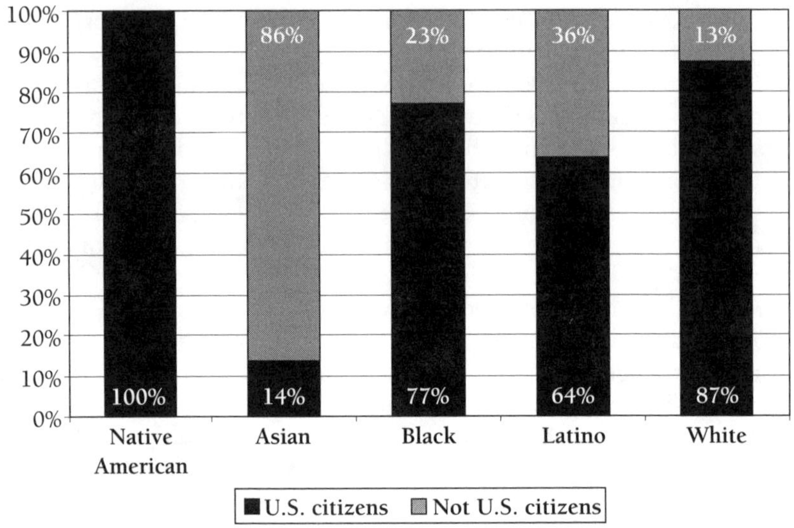

Source: American Council on Education, 2001.

Race, Ethnicity, and Class. The 1996–97 Minorities in Higher Education Report (Hune and Chan, 1997) indicated that aggregated data on Asian Americans homogenizes the experiences of Asians and provides a distorted picture of the educational participation of subgroups in the population. But in fact, the Asian American population is quite diverse, with ethnic, social class, and immigrant subgroups that encounter differing social and institutional experiences. One of the most apparent indications of the diversity among the umbrella racial category "Asian American and Pacific Islander" is the ethnic diversity (Teranishi, 2002). In 2000, the U.S. Census Bureau included forty-eight different Asian American and Pacific Islander categories to make up the AAPI racial population.

Across racial groups some populations have greater correlations between class and different outcomes than others. Among Asian Americans, there are correlations between ethnicity and class in the larger racial category that are lost in aggregated samples. For example, according to the U.S. Bureau of the Census (2000), Southeast Asians (for example, Laotians, Hmong, Cambodians, and Vietnamese) experience poverty rates that are two to four times greater than the national average. In 1990, 64 percent of Hmongs, 43 percent of Cambodians, and 35 percent of Laotians lived in poverty, in contrast to 30 percent of the black population and 28 percent of the Latino population nationally (see Figure 4.2). In comparative racial analysis, this trend would be overlooked among the Asian American popu-

Figure 4.2. Poverty Rates, by Race or Ethnicity, 1990

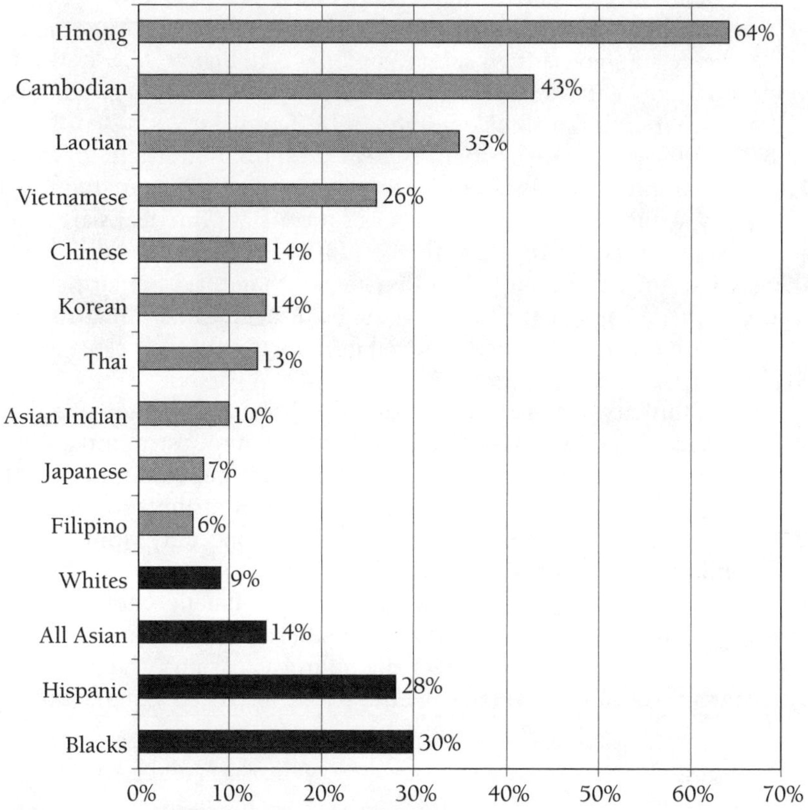

Group	Poverty Rate
Hmong	64%
Cambodian	43%
Laotian	35%
Vietnamese	26%
Chinese	14%
Korean	14%
Thai	13%
Asian Indian	10%
Japanese	7%
Filipino	6%
Whites	9%
All Asian	14%
Hispanic	28%
Blacks	30%

Source: U.S. Census Bureau, 2000.

lation. Arguably, similar distinctions within race are often hidden regarding subpopulations among Latinos, blacks, and whites.

It is often overlooked that Southeast Asians have the highest welfare dependency rates of any ethnic or racial group in the United States. Southeast Asians constitute nearly 80 percent of all Asian Americans on welfare. There are similar trends in employment rates among Asian Americans. In a study of Southeast Asian high school seniors in California, 49 percent of the fathers and 75 percent of mothers of Cambodian students were unemployed (Teranishi, 2004).

Another class indicator that is seldom associated with the Asian American population is educational attainment. Consistently, the perception of Asian Americans is that their educational attainment levels exceed all other racial groups in the nation. This perception masks wide differences in attainment that is found within ethnic groups. For example, a large proportion of Hmongs (59.6 percent), Cambodians (53.3 percent), Laotians (49.6 percent), and Vietnamese (38.1 percent) adults over the age of twenty-five do not have a high school diploma (see Figure 4.3). Low educational attainment among adults often results in a lack of college guidance and support for children (McDonough, 1997; Teranishi, 2003).

Beyond the ethnic diversity of the AAPI population, there are also a wide range of indicators and outcomes related to educational attainment and poverty status. In other words, just as some Asian Americans are at the top of the curve, many struggle at the bottom of the curve. The differences among Asian American groups are often greater than their similarities, and because of this Asian American data must be disaggregated to have meaning. Asian Americans are a unique racial group with unique needs, issues, and challenges.

Race, Ethnicity, and Family. Studies that use an aggregated sample of Asian American students mask the complexity of family structure, which varies widely across ethnicity and class. Among some populations of Southeast Asians, students assume adult roles in order to contribute to their families. A high proportion of Southeast Asians, and especially women, have been found to be caretakers or engaged in premature employment to support their families. The roles often vary by age placement among siblings (for example, number of younger and older siblings), gender, and differing levels of economic hardship. For female Southeast Asians, the pursuit of postsecondary education is often something to be balanced along with their

Figure 4.3. Proportion of Asian American Population Not Completing High School, by Ethnicity, 2000

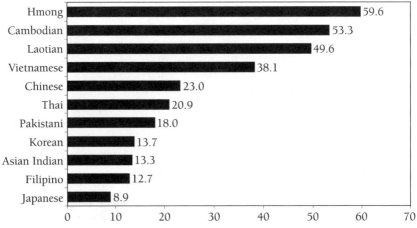

Source: U.S. Census Bureau, 2000.

NEW DIRECTIONS FOR INSTITUTIONAL RESEARCH • DOI: 10.1002/ir

adult roles and family obligations that are not traditionally practiced in the United States by other ethnic groups (Teranishi, 2003).

Another factor that is masked by cross-sectional racial frameworks is the mere drastic ranges of family composition for different subpopulations among Asian Americans. Families take many forms aside from the traditional nuclear construct. In the same study of Southeast Asians, we found that the Hmong student respondents had an average of 8.5 persons per household, with one student living in a household with 16 persons (Teranishi, 2003). For Hmong, the extremely high number of people in their homes can be partially attributed to family composition among Hmong culture. In many cases, the households of Hmong students included the immediate nuclear family (parents and children) in addition to grandparents, the wives of the sons in the family, and other relatives who needed support. In the Hmong culture, women often marry at a very early age. Our sample included female Hmong respondents who married at the ages of thirteen, fourteen, and fifteen.

Immigration Status, Nativity, and Language. Studies across race often overlook the differential experiences of immigrant versus native-born populations. For Asian Americans, who are the fastest-growing racial group in the nation, a larger proportion of the population is foreign-born. Even among the foreign-born population, there are differences in when they were likely to have arrived in the United States. For example, a large share of foreign-born Southeast Asians arrived here after 1980 (see Figure 4.4). This is an indicator

Figure 4.4. Foreign-Born Asian Americans, by Year of Entry and Ethnicity, 2000

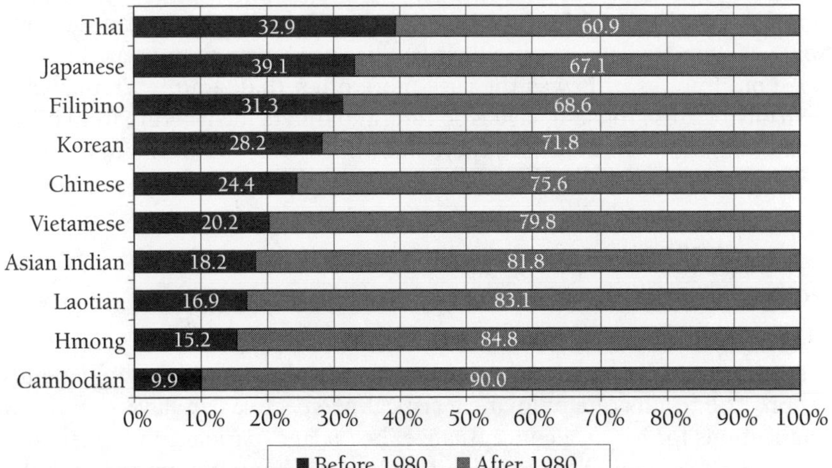

Ethnicity	Before 1980	After 1980
Thai	32.9	60.9
Japanese	39.1	67.1
Filipino	31.3	68.6
Korean	28.2	71.8
Chinese	24.4	75.6
Vietamese	20.2	79.8
Asian Indian	18.2	81.8
Laotian	16.9	83.1
Hmong	15.2	84.8
Cambodian	9.9	90.0

■ Before 1980   ■ After 1980

Source: U.S. Census Bureau, 2000.

NEW DIRECTIONS FOR INSTITUTIONAL RESEARCH • DOI: 10.1002/ir

Figure 4.5. English-Speaking Ability, by Ethnicity, 2000

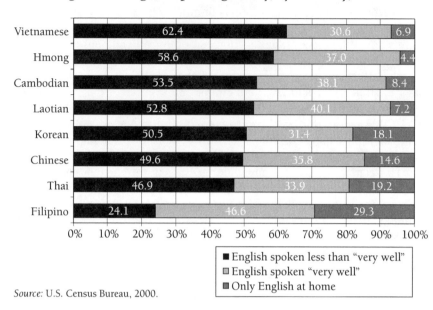

Source: U.S. Census Bureau, 2000.

of the populations who will face challenges associated with migration such as language, acculturation, and adjustment. Conversely, although a large portion of the Asian American population is first-generation, there are also many families who have been in the United States for generations. Nevertheless, they are treated as perpetual foreigners.

Among more recent immigrants, challenges are often associated with language. The likelihood that English is spoken at home for some groups is very low (see Figure 4.5). As a result students often feel they cannot leave home to attend college because their families need them to translate English.

For Hmongs, this was the case more often than among Vietnamese, probably because the language is so rare, and differs in structure from other Asian languages. In addition, there does not exist a written language for Hmongs.

The Need for Critical Perspectives in Stratified Designs

This chapter set out to demonstrate how a critical race theory framework can inform, guide, and design quantitative research on race in higher education. The results of employing a critical perspective can have significant implications for how we conceptualize the racial experience in higher education. Critical race theory challenges the most common approach to the way that we study racial populations, which has limitations for what we know about individual racial groups.

For the Asian American student population, traditional approaches to the study of race often promote and reinforce racialized assumptions that are held about Asian Americans based on studies that aggregate the population into a single racial category so they can be compared to other racial groups. As a result, research approaches to Asian Americans homogenize their experiences and offer a distorted picture of the educational participation of population subgroups. The perceived educational success of Asian Americans has resulted in their exclusion altogether from racial discourse on educational issues because it is believed that there is no need to address their educational issues.

This chapter raises important questions that should be considered when the study of race is a goal of a research design in higher education. It is important to consider the research questions that we will ask before a decision is made regarding the framework that will be employed to address them. What is the rationale for the questions being asked and the approach that will be taken to answer them? Are we trying to improve the educational conditions and outcomes for a particular student population or just demonstrate that a particular population is deficient or superior to others? Asking this type of question leads to broader questions about our motivation and leads to a choice from a variety of research approaches. If a quantitative method is the most appropriate approach, what is the utility of quantitative research and how can it best be used to address the questions that are being asked?

In addition to thinking carefully about crafting appropriate research questions, it is also important to consider the sampling procedure. What is our rationale for including different populations in our sample? What is gained by including different populations? When choosing populations for inclusion, exclusion is implicitly a concern. What do you lose by excluding various populations?

Targeting wide populations during sampling results in greater generalizability, but is that always the goal? Although generalizability is an important consideration in a quantitative design, it should be carefully considered in the study of race. Overcompensating for generalizability can take away from what we may be able to gain from learning about a specific population. In racial categories, homogeneity exists only to a certain extent. However, as described already, racial categories as a whole are not consistently homogeneous across groups with regard to their characteristics. Therefore, we cannot assume that there is enough consistency in the homogeneity across racial groups that they are equally comparable.

Research questions should lead to consideration of sampling procedures that will yield the information necessary to inform the results of the study. Identifying extraneous factors and discussing how these may or may not affect a study is critical to the validity of the results. In the case of the Asian American population, important distinctions among subpopulations must be considered. For example, the Asian American population is diverse in ethnic, social class, and immigrant subgroups that encounter different social and institutional experiences. For the study of Asian Americans in higher education, it is also important to consider such factors as migration and settlement of the population, the correlation between class and the particular ethnicity that is being studied, and how culture affects men and women differently.

More research that is able to highlight these distinctions and problematize "race" in research will improve the ways in which we develop policies and services that assist all students in their access to and success in higher education.

References

Allen, W. "Missing in Action: Race, Gender, and Black Students' Educational Opportunities." In Devon W. Carbado (ed.), *Black Men on Race, Gender, and Sexuality: A Critical Reader* (pp. 194–211). New York: New York University Press, 1999.

Bell, D. *And We Will Not Be Saved: The Elusive Quest for Racial Justice.* New York: Basic Books, 1987.

Bowen, W., Kurzweil, M., and Tobin, E. *Equity and Excellence in American Higher Education.* Charlottesville: University of Virginia Press, 2005.

Carrasco, E. "Collective Recognition as a Communitarian Device: Or, of Course We Want to Be Role Models!" *La Raza Law Journal,* 1996, *9,* 81–101.

Carter, D. J., and Wilson, R. *Eighth Annual Status Report on Minorities in Higher Education.* Washington, D.C.: American Council on Education, 1989.

Chang, R. S. *Disoriented: Asian Americans, Law, and the Nation-State.* New York: New York University Press, 1999.

Delgado, R. "Storytelling for Oppositionalists and Others: A Plea for Narrative." *Michigan Law Review,* 1989, *87,* 2411–2441.

Delgado, R. *Critical Race Theory: The Cutting Edge.* Philadelphia: Temple University Press, 1995.

Garcia, R. "Critical Race Theory and Proposition 187: The Racial Politics of Immigration Law." *Chicano-Latino Law Review,* 1995, *17,* 118–148.

Harris, A. "Foreword: The Jurisprudence of Reconstruction." *California Law Review,* 1994, *82,* 741–785.

Hune, S. "Demographics and Diversity of Asian American College Students." In M. McEwen, C. Kodama, A. Alvarez, and C. Liang (eds.), *Working with Asian American College Students* (pp. 11–20). San Francisco: Jossey-Bass, 2002.

Hune, S., and Chan, K. S. "Special Focus: Asian Pacific American Demographics and Educational Trends." In D. Carter and R. Wilson (eds.), *Minorities in Higher Education.* Vol. 15. Washington, D.C.: American Council on Education, 1997.

Kim, C. J. "The Racial Triangulation of Asian Americans." *Politics and Society,* 1999, *27,* 105–138.

McDonough, P. M. *Choosing Colleges: How Social Class and Schools Structure Opportunity.* Albany: State University of New York Press, 1997.

Nakanishi, D. T. "Asian/Pacific Americans and Selective Undergraduate Admissions." *Journal of College Admissions,* 1995, *118,* 17–26.

Olivas, M. "The Chronicles, My Grandfather's Stories, and Immigration Law: The Slave Traders' Chronicle as Racial History." *St. Louis University Law Journal,* 1990, *34,* 425–441.

NEW DIRECTIONS FOR INSTITUTIONAL RESEARCH • DOI: 10.1002/ir

Solórzano, D. G. "Critical Race Theory, Race and Gender Microaggressions, and the Experience of Chicana and Chicano Scholars." *Qualitative Studies in Education,* 1998, *11*(1), 121–136.

Solórzano, D., and Villalpando, O. "Critical Race Theory, Marginality, and the Experience of Minority Students in Higher Education." In C. A. Torres and T. R. Mitchell (eds.), *Sociology of Education: Emerging Perspectives* (pp. 211–224), Albany: State University of New York Press, 1998.

Solórzano, D., Villalpando, O., and Oseguera, L. "Educational Inequities and Latina/o Undergraduate Students in the United States: A Critical Race Analysis of Their Educational Progress." *Journal of Hispanic Higher Education,* 2005, *4,* 272–294.

Stanton-Salazar, R. D., and Spina, S. U. "The Network Orientations of Highly Resilient Urban Minority Youth: A Network-Analytic Account of Minority Socialization and Its Educational Implications." *Urban Review,* 2001, *32*(3), 227–261.

Takagi, D. Y. *The Retreat from Race: Asian-American Admissions and Racial Politics.* New Brunswick, N.J.: Rutgers University Press, 1992.

Tate, W. "Critical Race Theory and Education: History, Theory and Implications." *Review of Research in Education,* 1997, *22,* 191–243.

Teranishi, R. "Myth of the Super Minority: Misconceptions About Asian Americans." *College Board Review,* 2002, *195,* 16–21.

Teranishi, R. "'Raced' Perspectives on College Opportunity: Examining Asian Americans Through Critical Race Theory." *Equity and Excellence in Education,* 2003, *35*(2), 144–154.

Teranishi, R. "Yellow and Brown: Residential Segregation and Emerging Asian American Immigrant Populations." *Equity and Excellence in Education,* 2004, *37*(3), 255–263.

Teranishi, R. *Asian American and Pacific Islander Participation in U.S. Higher Education: Status and Trends.* New York: College Board, 2005a.

Teranishi, R. *Normative Approaches to Policy Research in Education: Implications for Asian Americans and Pacific Islanders.* New York: College Board, 2005b.

Thurgood, L., Golloday, M., and Hill, S. *U.S. Doctorates in the 20th Century.* Washington, D.C.: National Science Foundation, 2006.

U.S. Bureau of the Census. *Summary File 1.* Washington, D.C.: U.S. Census Bureau, 2000.

Zia, H. *Asian/Pacific Americans and Higher Education: Facts, Not Fiction—Setting the Record Straight.* New York: College Board, 2006.

ROBERT T. TERANISHI *is assistant professor of higher education at New York University and codirector of the National Commission on Asian American and Pacific Islander Research in Education. He is also a faculty affiliate with the Steinhardt Institute for Higher Education Policy and the Alliance for International Higher Education Policy Studies.*

5

The chapter begins by discussing why the continued underrepresentation of blacks and Hispanics in American higher education is a critical area for research, policy, and practice. The author then describes the expanded conceptual model and summarizes research support for the model.

The Sources of Racial-Ethnic Group Differences in College Enrollment: A Critical Examination

Laura W. Perna

A review of the wide body of research on college enrollment suggests that, traditionally, researchers who employ an economic theoretical perspective (for example, Manski and Wise, 1983; Heller, 1999; Kane, 1999) or status attainment theoretical perspective (for example, Sewell, Hauser, and Wolf, 1986; Hearn, 1991) use quantitative methods, whereas researchers who focus on the roles of cultural and social capital (for example, McDonough, 1997) use qualitative methods. Yet efforts to incorporate measures of cultural and social capital into a traditional economic approach to college enrollment result in models that better explain the decisions of students to enroll in both undergraduate and postbaccalaureate education (for example, Perna, 2000, 2004, 2006). An approach that uses quantitative analyses of large-scale nationwide databases and a conceptual model that integrates economic and sociological constructs may be particularly useful for understanding the sources of observed racial and ethnic group differences in enrollment patterns (Perna, 2006).

This chapter begins by discussing why the continued underrepresentation of blacks and Hispanics in American higher education is a critical area for research, policy, and practice. The chapter then describes an expanded conceptual model and summarizes research support for the model. The strengths and weaknesses of using quantitative analyses to address this critical policy question are identified next. The chapter

NEW DIRECTIONS FOR INSTITUTIONAL RESEARCH, no. 133, Spring 2007 © Wiley Periodicals, Inc.
Published online in Wiley InterScience (www.interscience.wiley.com) • DOI: 10.1002/ir.204

concludes by recommending the use of quantitative analyses of an integrated conceptual model to gain additional insights about the sources of continued racial-ethnic group gaps in college enrollment.

Critical Policy Issue

Understanding the sources of racial-ethnic group differences in college enrollment is critical for several reasons. First, African Americans and Hispanics continue to average lower levels of educational attainment than whites. Second, racial-ethnic group differences in educational attainment contribute to the persisting economic and social stratification of American society by race and ethnicity. Third, gaps in college enrollment continue despite the existence of several policy interventions. Finally, particularly in light of the previous three conclusions, a review of prior research suggests that a more comprehensive conceptual model is required to explain differences across racial and ethnic groups in college enrollment processes and outcomes.

Persisting Racial-Ethnic Group Differences in Educational Attainment. Although educational attainment rates have generally increased over the past thirty years (U.S. Department of Education, 2006), African Americans and Hispanics continue to average lower levels of educational attainment than whites. Numerous sources demonstrate the lower educational attainment for African Americans and Hispanics. For example, data from the March 2005 *Current Population Survey* show that a higher share of whites ages twenty-five and older than of blacks and Hispanics in the same age group had completed at least a bachelor's degree (31 percent versus 18 percent and 12 percent). The racial-ethnic group gap in educational attainment persists even when only relatively younger individuals are considered. For example, among those who were between the ages of twenty-five and twenty-nine in March 2005, 34 percent of whites but only 18 percent of blacks and 11 percent of Hispanics had completed at least a bachelor's degree (U.S. Department of Education, 2006).

Analyses of data that track the educational progress of a cohort of students over time also demonstrate the racial-ethnic group gap in educational attainment. Data from the High School and Beyond longitudinal study of 1980 high school sophomores show that by 1992—ten years after most 1980 high school sophomores graduated from high school—more than one-fourth (28 percent) of whites had completed at least a bachelor's degree, compared with only 12 percent of blacks and 10 percent of Hispanics (U.S. Department of Education, 2002b). Data from a more recent longitudinal study, the National Educational Longitudinal Study of 1988 eighth graders (NELS:88), suggest that, although degree attainment rates have increased for all groups, the racial-ethnic gap in educational attainment remains. By 2000—eight years after most 1988 eighth graders graduated from high school—35 percent of whites had completed at least a bachelor's degree compared with only 17 percent of blacks and 15 percent of Hispanics (U.S. Department of Education, 2003).

NEW DIRECTIONS FOR INSTITUTIONAL RESEARCH • DOI: 10.1002/ir

Table 5.1. Percent Distribution of Enrollments and Degree Recipients by Race or Ethnicity, 2004

Status	Total	White	Black	Hispanic	Asian	American Indian	Nonresident
Undergraduate enrollment	100.0	66.1	13.0	11.3	6.4	1.1	2.1
Associate degree	100.0	67.2	13.6	11.0	4.7	1.3	2.2
Bachelor's degree	100.0	73.3	9.4	6.8	6.6	0.8	3.2
Master's degree	100.0	66.1	9.1	5.3	5.5	0.6	13.4
First-professional degree	100.0	72.7	7.1	5.1	12.0	0.7	2.3
Doctoral degree	100.0	58.3	6.0	3.4	5.4	0.4	26.4

Note: Undergraduate enrollment is total undergraduate enrollment in fall 2004. Completions data are for the 2003–04 academic year.

Source: U.S. Department of Education, 2006.

Annual completions data from the U.S. Department of Education's Common Core of Data and Integrated Postsecondary Education Data System provide yet another indicator of racial-ethnic group gaps in educational attainment. Table 5.1 shows that the representation of blacks and Hispanics declines as the level of educational attainment increases. Specifically, blacks received 13.6 percent of all associate degrees, 9.4 percent of all bachelor's degrees, 9.1 percent of all master's degrees, 7.1 percent of all first-professional degrees, and 6.0 percent of all doctorates that were awarded in 2003–04 (U.S. Department of Education, 2006). Similarly, Hispanics represented 11.0 percent of associate degree, 6.8 percent of bachelor's degree, 5.3 percent of master's degree, 5.1 percent of first-professional degree, and 3.4 percent of doctoral degree recipients.

Consequences of Racial-Ethnic Group Differences in Educational Attainment. Persisting differences in educational attainment across racial-ethnic groups are problematic, at least in part because they contribute to the economic and social stratification of American society. The observed racial-ethnic group differences in educational attainment suggest that African Americans and Hispanics are less likely than whites to realize the economic, social, and other benefits that are associated with higher education. An individual who participates in higher education realizes not only such short-term consumption benefits as enjoyment of the learning experience, involvement in extracurricular activities, participation in social and cultural events, and enhancement of social status but also such long-term economic and social benefits as greater cognitive learning, greater emotional and moral development, more fringe benefits, improved working conditions, more appropriate investment and saving, improved health, longer life, lower likelihood of unemployment, lower likelihood of disability, more leisure time, more informed purchases, greater citizenship, and higher spousal income (Bowen, 1997; Leslie and Brinkman, 1988; McPherson, 1993).

An increase in earnings is the most readily observed individual benefit of higher education. In 2005, median earnings of full-time, year-round workers between the ages of thirty-five and forty-four were substantially higher for individuals who attained a bachelor's degree ($54,800) or advanced degree ($72,200) than for those who completed only high school ($32,200; College Board, 2006b). Estimated lifetime earnings in 2003 were 73 percent higher for those with a bachelor's degree (excluding those who also earned advanced degrees of any kind) than for those with only a high school diploma (Baum and Payea, 2004).

As others (for example, Perna, 2003) point out, considering only the observed difference in earnings between individuals who earn a bachelor's degree and individuals who earn a high school diploma likely overestimates the private monetary benefits of attending college. Specifically, individuals who attain a bachelor's degree may have higher earnings in part because they have greater academic ability and higher levels of motivation than individuals who attain only a high school diploma. Nonetheless, even after controlling for differences in other variables, the earnings premium that is associated with completing a bachelor's degree rather than a high school diploma is substantial (Leslie and Brinkman, 1988; Perna, 2003). Based on their integrative review of thirteen studies, Leslie and Brinkman (1988) concluded that 79 percent of the observed difference in earnings between college and high school graduates is attributable to attending and graduating from college. Although some research (Monks, 2000) suggests that earnings are higher for nonwhites than for whites after controlling for other variables, other research (Perna, 2003) shows that the earnings premium associated with attaining a bachelor's degree rather than a high school diploma is comparable across racial-ethnic groups.

Occupational status also increases with educational attainment. Data from the U.S. Census Bureau (2001) show that about two-thirds of managerial and professional positions are held by individuals who hold at least a bachelor's degree among both men (67 percent) and women (61 percent). Fewer than one in seven managerial and professional positions are held by workers who have completed no more than a high school diploma. College graduates represent only a small fraction of male precision production workers (7 percent), male operators and fabricators (6 percent), female service workers (7 percent), and female operators and fabricators (4 percent).

A bachelor's degree is increasingly the minimum acceptable educational credential for many employers. A bachelor's degree was required for 29 percent of all jobs in 2000 and is expected to be required for 42 percent of all new jobs that are created by 2010 (U.S. Department of Labor, 2002). The Bureau of Labor Statistics reports that twelve of the twenty fastest-growing occupations generally require a bachelor's or associate degree (U.S. Department of Labor, 2003).

New Directions for Institutional Research • DOI: 10.1002/ir

Existing Policies and Practices Have Not Eliminated Differences in College Enrollment. One source of observed differences in educational attainment is racial-ethnic group differences in college enrollment. Smaller shares of blacks and Hispanics than of whites who completed high school in 2004 enrolled in college in the fall after completing high school (63 percent and 62 percent versus 69 percent; U.S. Department of Education, 2006). Moreover, blacks and Hispanics who do enroll are more likely than whites to attend for-profit postsecondary educational institutions than public and private, not-for-profit two-year and four-year colleges and universities. Specifically, higher shares of black and Hispanic first-time, full-time, first-year students than of white and Asian first-time, full-time, first-year students attended for-profit institutions in 2004 (14 percent and 14 percent versus 6 percent and 5 percent, respectively; College Board, 2006b).

The primary public policy vehicle for addressing gaps in college access and choice is student financial aid. The federal government, state governments, colleges and universities, private organizations, and employers awarded nearly $135 billion to postsecondary education students in the form of financial aid (including federal education tax benefits) in 2005–06. The federal government is the largest source of student financial aid, with federally sponsored programs representing 70 percent of the total $135 billion in financial aid that was awarded in 2005–06 (College Board, 2006a).

Despite the substantial investment in student financial aid by the federal government and other entities, the data described here show that racial-ethnic group gaps in college enrollment remain. The persistence of these gaps suggests that, as others (for example, Gladieux and Swail, 1999) have concluded, financial aid is not enough. In other words, eliminating gaps in college enrollment requires attention not only to the financial barriers to college enrollment but also to the academic, social, and psychological barriers.

Through early intervention or precollege outreach programs, numerous entities, including the federal government, state governments, private nonprofit organizations, foundations, and colleges and universities, recognize that college access and choice are limited not only by financial barriers but also by barriers that are associated with inadequate academic preparation, knowledge of college requirements, costs, and financial aid, and assistance from teachers, counselors, family members, and peers (Swail and Perna, 2002). These programs are designed to provide students from groups that have been historically underrepresented in higher education (for example, students from low-income families, potential first-generation college students, blacks, and Hispanics) with the opportunity to develop, early in the educational pipeline, the college-related skills, knowledge, aspirations, and preparation that are required for postsecondary enrollment and attainment. The federal programs include the TRIO programs (such as Upward Bound), student-based early intervention programs, and the Gaining Early Awareness and Readiness for Undergraduate Program (GEAR-UP), a school-based approach to early intervention.

NEW DIRECTIONS FOR INSTITUTIONAL RESEARCH • DOI: 10.1002/ir

Despite the prevalence of these programs, little is known about their effectiveness overall or of particular programmatic components (Tierney, 2002). The best available evidence, the federally sponsored evaluation of Upward Bound, suggests that this program has a small but statistically significant impact, especially on four-year college enrollment rates (Myers, Olsen, Seftor, Young, and Tuttle, 2004). The evaluation also shows that Upward Bound is especially beneficial to Hispanics, as well as to individuals who had low educational expectations when they applied to the program and those who were both from low-income families and potential first-generation college students. Although this evaluation suggests that the program, in the aggregate, promotes particular college-related outcomes and is especially effective for Hispanics and students from other groups, the evaluation does not shed light on the contribution of particular or specific programmatic activities to these outcomes.

To eliminate the observed racial-ethnic group gaps in college enrollment, policymakers and practitioners must better understand the sources of the persisting gaps and the programmatic activities that effectively address these gaps. More comprehensive analyses of the college enrollment process are required to better understand the ways students of different racial and ethnic groups make decisions about attending college. The results of these analyses can be used to guide policymakers and program administrators in their efforts to reduce persisting gaps in college access and choice.

Need for a More Comprehensive Conceptual Model for Examining Group Differences in College Enrollment. Quantitative researchers have traditionally relied on sociological status attainment models and economic models of decision making to examine the predictors of college enrollment. Sociological status attainment models focus on the ways that interactions between a student and his or her parents, peers, teachers, and others shape educational outcomes (Hossler, Schmit, and Vesper, 1999; McDonough, 1997). Status attainment models are primarily concerned with the effects of socioeconomic status (SES) on educational aspirations and attainment (McDonough, 1997).

A traditional economic perspective assumes that individuals make decisions by weighing the costs against the benefits for all possible alternatives and then selecting the alternative that maximizes utility with respect to individual preferences, tastes, and expectations (Manski and Wise, 1983). Quantitative research that uses an economic perspective generally focuses on the extent to which student financial aid reduces differences in college enrollment. Research consistently shows that student financial aid promotes college enrollment (St. John, 1991), regardless of whether the aid is in the form of grants, loans, or work-study (St. John and Noell, 1989). African American and low-income students appear to be particularly sensitive to the availability of financial aid (Jackson, 1990; Heller, 1997).

McDonough (1997) illustrates the limitations of traditional status attainment and economic approaches to college enrollment. Using rich case studies and cross-case analyses, McDonough shows that students consider a restricted set of postsecondary options and that these options are largely determined by the context of the schools they attend and their family social class context. Through the structure of college guidance activities, the college-related mission and curriculum, assumptions about students' cultural capital, and guidance counselor roles and behaviors, the school shapes students' college choice processes, structuring a student's postsecondary educational expectations and the set of options that a student considers. McDonough (1997) also demonstrates the ways in which college choice processes vary across social classes. The college choice processes of students from lower and higher SES families differ in part because of differences in the availability of external resources (for example, attendance at a private school, use of a private college counselor) and in terms of the constraints a family places on the choice process (for example, geographic limits, financial constraints) and the consistency of the messages that students receive about college.

Although McDonough's conclusions (1997) are drawn from case studies of only four high schools in one state, other recent qualitative research illustrates the importance of considering the influence of the organizational context in general, and cultural and social capital in particular, when examining the college enrollment behavior of African Americans and Hispanics. Through interviews with African American high school students about the barriers they perceive to African Americans' participation in higher education, Freeman (1997) found that African American students were uncertain about their ability to pay the short-term costs of attending and about whether the long-term economic benefits of attending would exceed the costs. Interviewees also pointed to the potential influence of the physical conditions of the schools attended by African Americans, interest and assistance from teachers and counselors, believing at an early age that pursuing postsecondary education is a realistic option, and African American role models. Based on her qualitative study of educational attainment among African American and Mexican American valedictorians, Arnold (1993) concluded that racial, class, and gendered social structures and cultural norms restrict educational attainment for minority students.

An Integrated Conceptual Model

Although economic approaches ostensibly recognize that cost-benefit analyses occur in the context of individual preferences, tastes, and expectations, in practice researchers who adopt an economic approach attempt to account for differences in preferences, tastes, and expectations only by including measures of students' sex, race, parental education, and academic ability. A rational human capital investment model assumes that, even when the expected benefits and costs are the same, two individuals may make different college choices because of differences in their preferences, tolerance for risk, and uncertainty (DesJardins and Toutkoushian, 2005). But measures

NEW DIRECTIONS FOR INSTITUTIONAL RESEARCH • DOI: 10.1002/ir

of preferences, tolerance for risk, and uncertainty are generally omitted from economic models.

Moreover, traditional economic approaches do not attempt to incorporate the forces that constrain decision-making processes. Human capital models do not assume that individuals have perfect and complete information but evaluate college options based on available information about the benefits and costs (DesJardins and Toutkoushian, 2005). However, potential students not only lack information about college opportunities but also have differential access to information (Kane, 1999). College enrollment decision-making processes are also constrained by cognitive, time, and resource limitations, as well as by family preferences and knowledge and school policies and structures (for example, the availability of college counseling; McDonough, 1997, 2005).

Recognizing these limitations, some researchers (Paulsen and St. John, 2002; Perna, 2000, 2004, 2006; St. John and Asker, 2001) argue that traditional economic approaches be expanded to include measures of social and cultural capital as proxies for individual expectations, preferences, tastes, and uncertainty about the enrollment decision. Based on her comprehensive review and synthesis of prior research, Perna (2006) proposed a conceptual model that integrates aspects of the economic theory of human capital and sociological notions of social and cultural capital. The model also recognizes that multiple layers of context influence an individual's college-related decision making by providing access to different resources and opportunities. The four layers of context in the model are the individual's habitus, the school and community context, the higher education context, and the social, economic, and policy context.

Reflecting human capital theory, Perna's integrated conceptual model (2006) assumes that college-related decisions are based on a comparison of the expected benefits with the expected costs. The expected benefits include both monetary and nonmonetary benefits, whereas the expected costs include the costs of attendance and forgone earnings. Also like human capital investment models, Perna's model assumes that calculations of the expected benefits and costs are influenced by an individual's academic preparation for college and availability of resources to pay the costs of attendance.

Unlike traditional economic approaches, Perna's conceptual model (2006) assumes that the college enrollment decision-making process takes place in the context of an individual's habitus, as well as other layers of context. *Habitus* is the internalized set of dispositions and preferences that subconsciously define an individual's reasonable actions (Bourdieu and Wacquant, 1992; McDonough, 1997) or the system of values and beliefs that shapes an individual's views and interpretations (Paulsen and St. John, 2002; St. John and Asker, 2001).

Although economic approaches focus on the roles of financial and academic resources, an integrated conceptual model assumes that individuals may draw on multiple forms of capital in the college enrollment process, including financial, human, cultural, and social capital. Like other forms of capital, cultural and social capital are resources that individuals may draw on as needed to enhance productivity (Coleman, 1988), facilitate upward mobility (DiMaggio and Mohr, 1985; Lamont and Lareau, 1988), and realize economic returns (Lin, 2001). One way cultural and social capital may influence expectations, preferences, and uncertainty about enrollment is through the provision of knowledge and information about the costs and benefits (DiMaggio and Mohr, 1985; McDonough, 1997).

Perna's proposed model (2006) also explicitly recognizes the roles of other layers of context in shaping college-related decisions. For example, drawing on McDonough's research (1997), the school and community context layer of the model recognizes the role of social structures and resources in shaping college-related behaviors. Attention to the higher education context recognizes that higher education institutions may influence students' college-related behaviors by actively and passively providing information to students about college. The social, economic, and policy layer of the model recognizes the contribution of such public policies as financial aid and tuition and other forces to students' college-related behaviors (Perna, 2006).

Research Support for the Model

Quantitative research supports both the integration of economic and sociological perspectives into a model of college enrollment (for example, Perna, 2000, 2004) and the inclusion of multiple layers of context for understanding racial and ethnic group differences in college enrollment (for example, Perna and Titus, 2005).

Using data from the National Educational Longitudinal Study, Perna (2000) found that the lower observed rates of four-year college enrollment for Hispanics and African Americans than for whites were explained by racial-ethnic group differences in measures of costs and benefits, academic ability, and cultural and social capital. Specifically, four-year college enrollment rates were comparable for Hispanics and whites after controlling for other variables in the model. Like some prior research (for example, Kane and Spizman, 1994), Perna (2000) also found that, after controlling for differences in other variables, African Americans were about 11 percentage points more likely than whites to enroll in a four-year college or university in the fall after graduating from high school. Like others (Hurtado, Inkelas, Briggs, and Rhee, 1997), Perna cautions that only a small number of African Americans are "equal" to whites in terms of all other characteristics. Also like some other research (for example, Jackson, 1990; St. John, 1991), Perna found that several independent variables interacted with race and ethnicity, suggesting that the predictors of enrolling in a four-year college or university immediately after graduating from high school are different for African Americans and Hispanics than for whites.

Besides showing that an expanded economic model explains the sources of observed racial-ethnic group differences in four-year college enrollment, Perna (2000) also found that adding measures of cultural and social capital to a traditional economic model of college enrollment significantly improved the fit of the model for whites, African Americans, and Hispanics. Her analyses suggest that measures of cultural and social capital are particularly important to the decision of African Americans and Hispanics to enroll in a four-year college. Specifically, for African Americans and Hispanics, the contribution of the measures of cultural and social capital to the logistic regression model was comparable in magnitude to the contribution of measures of academic ability and achievement. For whites, the contribution was greater for the measures of academic ability and achievement than for the measures of cultural and social capital. Measures of cultural and social capital included characteristics of the high school that may be related to the knowledge and information available to students (for example, quality, racial-ethnic composition, location, control, geographic region), indicators of the extent to which a student values higher education (such as parental encouragement, parental involvement in the child's education, the student's educational expectations), and social networks and resources (such as peer encouragement for college enrollment, encouragement from a teacher or counselor to go to college).

Using data from the Baccalaureate and Beyond Study of 1993 (B&B:93) bachelor's degree recipients, Perna (2004) demonstrated the usefulness of an integrated conceptual model for understanding the sources of observed racial-ethnic group differences in postbaccalaureate enrollment. Although the multinomial logistic regression analyses suggested the sources of observed sex differences in submaster's level and master's degree enrollment, the analyses did not explain the lower observed representation of women than men among doctoral and first-professional program enrollees or the higher observed representation of Asians than of other racial-ethnic groups among first-professional enrollees. Nonetheless, Perna found that adding measures of cultural and social capital to the model improved several indicators of fit, including the ratio of scaled deviance to degrees of freedom, the pseudo-R^2, and the percentage of cases correctly classified. Measures of cultural capital included parental educational attainment, primary language spoken in the home, parental education, the extent to which an individual values being successful in the labor market, and the extent to which an individual values various aspects of future work. Social capital was measured by parental involvement (for example, the monetary contribution that bachelor's degree recipients received from their parents for their undergraduate education) and characteristics of the bachelor's degree–granting institution that may reflect the existence of social networks that may promote graduate enrollment (for example, Carnegie classification, tuition, and location).

Other research shows the value of quantitative analyses for understanding the contribution of different layers of context to differences in college enrollment across racial and ethnic groups (Perna and Titus, 2005). Focusing on parental involvement as a form of social capital, Perna and Titus used hierarchical linear modeling to show that likelihood of enrolling in a two-year or four-year college after graduating from high school is related to the volume of resources (for example, the amount of social capital) that may be accessed through social networks at the school attended. In other words, the analyses show that the positive effects of school-level measures of parental involvement and other measures of social capital on college enrollment occur over and above the positive effects of an individual's level of parental involvement. Like Perna (2000), Perna and Titus found that the predictors of college enrollment vary across racial-ethnic groups. For example, parental involvement in the form of parent-school contact about academics had a greater effect on four-year college enrollment for African Americans than for whites, whereas parental involvement in the form of parent-student discussions about education issues had a smaller effect. Unlike for whites, the odds of enrolling in a four-year college decline for African Americans as perceptions of controllable costs (measured by the importance of living at home to attend college) increase.

Strengths and Weaknesses of Quantitative Analyses to Address This Critical Question

Research that uses quantitative analyses to develop and test an integrated and multilevel model of college enrollment has both strengths and weaknesses. Among the strengths are the external validity of the results, the high statistical power, and the range of available variables. The weaknesses include the possibility of inadequate proxies and omitted variables, the small numbers of some groups in the sample, and the age of the data.

Strengths of Quantitative Analyses. One strength of quantitative analyses, especially studies that use the large-scale longitudinal databases that are sponsored by the U.S. Department of Education, is the external validity. For example, several of the studies already cited (Perna, 2000; Perna and Titus, 2005) use the National Educational Longitudinal Study of 1988 eighth graders. Sponsored by the U.S. Department of Education, the NELS tracks the educational experiences of a cohort of students over time, with data collections when most students were in the eighth grade (1988), tenth grade (1990), twelfth grade (1992), two years out of high school (1994), and eight years out of high school (2000). Several features of the NELS:88 help ensure the generalizability of the results. First, the study is characterized by high response rates. For example, 14,915 of the 15,875 selected students (94 percent unweighted response rate; 91 percent weighted) completed the third follow-up survey in 1994, two years after most students had left high school (U.S. Department of Education, 2002a). NCES also developed a series of weights that allow a researcher to easily adjust for the probability that a student is selected in the sample, nonresponse, and sampling error. Thus, when the appropriate weight is applied, the data are representative of the population of students nationwide.

A second strength is the statistical power to detect differences. Because of the large number of total cases, the oversampling of Asians and Hispanics, and the high response rates, the NELS has a sufficient number of cases to allow detailed examinations of the college enrollment–related experiences of African Americans and Hispanics.

A third strength of this line of research is the availability of data to develop and test an integrated conceptual model. The NELS allows a researcher to examine not only the college enrollment process over time (that is, from the eighth grade to eight years after high school graduation) but also the ways in which parents, teachers, and the school influence the decision-making process. The NELS includes five waves of data from students (1988, 1990, 1992, 1994, and 2000), two waves of data from parents (1988 and 1990), three waves of data from school administrators (1988, 1990, and 1992), three waves of data from teachers (1988, 1990, and 1992), three waves of cognitive test results (1988, 1990, and 1992), and two waves of transcript data (1992 and 2000). The NELS data are particularly useful for multilevel analyses that explore the ways in which the school context—particularly the social networks in a student's high school—influence students' college enrollment behavior (Perna and Titus, 2005).

Challenges for Quantitative Analyses. One challenge facing researchers who attempt to develop and test an integrated model of college enrollment using quantitative analyses is to ensure the adequacy of proxies for complex theoretical constructs. Identifying appropriate proxies for aspects of cultural and social capital is particularly challenging. For example, both Perna (2000) and Perna and Titus (2005) assume that parental involvement in a child's education is a critical form of social capital. Yet, although the NELS:88 database has a number of variables that are reported by both the student and the parent that pertain to parental involvement, the available measures reflect only the quantity and not the quality of interactions between a parent and child (Dika and Singh, 2002; Perna and Titus, 2005) and traditional forms of involvement (for example, "parental" rather than "family" involvement) with no attention to the role of older siblings and members of the extended family. Such "nontraditional" involvement may be an especially important source of social capital for minority students (Tierney and Auerbach, 2005). Perna's (2004) examination of graduate school enrollment is limited by the paucity of variables in the B&B database to measure the social networks that a bachelor's degree recipient developed as an undergraduate and that may promote enrollment in graduate school.

A second challenge facing quantitative researchers is the ability to understand the experiences of some racial-ethnic groups (such as American Indian and Alaskan Natives) and the experiences of subgroups of some racial-ethnic groups (particularly Hispanics and Asians). Most existing databases, including those that the U.S. Department of Education sponsors, include insufficient numbers to perform detailed quantitative examinations of the college enrollment experiences of American Indian and Alaskan Natives or subgroups within the heterogeneous Hispanic and Asian categories.

Finally, both quantitative and qualitative researchers are challenged to understand the predictors of college enrollment for different groups given changes over time in public policies, societal values, economic conditions, and other characteristics. The NELS describes the college enrollment process for students who were high school seniors in 1992. If college enrollment processes are influenced by the economic, social, and political context (as predicted in Perna's 2006 conceptual model), and if this context has changed over time, then the applicability of the findings from this database to today's high school seniors is restricted. Fortunately, the U.S. Department of Education has responded to this challenge by sponsoring longitudinal surveys that, taken together, allow researchers to assess changes over time in college enrollment processes. The NELS describes the college enrollment behavior of students in the 1990s, whereas earlier U.S. Department of Education studies provide longitudinal data on the college enrollment experiences of students in the 1970s (the National Longitudinal Study of the High School Class of 1972) and the 1980s (the High School and Beyond Study of 1980 high school sophomores). Also sponsored by the U.S. Department of Education, the Educational Longitudinal Study of 2002 (ELS) describes the educational experiences of students in the 2000s (U.S. Department of Education, 2002a).

Conclusions

Despite the limitations, quantitative analyses can be used to address the critical policy question: Why do African Americans and Hispanics continue to be underrepresented in American higher education? Quantitative analyses are especially useful for identifying the magnitude of this critical problem, testing an integrated conceptual model for understanding the problem, raising questions that should be addressed via additional quantitative and qualitative research, and identifying ways in which future large-scale data collections (for example, ELS) can be improved to provide more appropriate measures of constructs that have been historically measured qualitatively—such as cultural and social capital.

References

Arnold, K. D. "The Fulfillment of Promise: Minority Valedictorians and Salutatorians." *Review of Higher Education,* 1993, *16*(3), 257–283.

Baum, S., and Payea, K. *Education Pays 2004: The Benefits of Higher Education for Individuals and Society.* Washington, D.C.: College Board, 2004.

Bourdieu, P., and Wacquant, L.J.D. *An Invitation to Reflexive Sociology.* Chicago: University of Chicago Press, 1992.

Bowen, H. R. *Investment in Learning: The Individual and Social Value of American Higher Education.* Baltimore: Johns Hopkins University Press, 1997.

Coleman, J. S. "Social Capital in the Creation of Human Capital." *American Journal of Sociology,* 1988, *94* (Supplement), 95–120.

College Board. *Trends in Student Aid 2006.* Washington, D.C.: College Board, 2006a.

College Board. *Education Pays, Second Update: A Supplement to Education Pays 2004.* Washington, D.C.: College Board, 2006b.

DesJardins, S. L., and Toutkoushian, R. K. "Are Students Really Rational? The Development of Rational Thought and Its Application to Student Choice." In J. C. Smart (ed.), *Higher Education: Handbook of Theory and Research,* Vol. 20 (pp. 191–240). Dordrecht, The Netherlands: Kluwer Academic, 2005.

Dika, S. L., and Singh, K. "Applications of Social Capital in Educational Literature: A Critical Synthesis." *Review of Educational Research,* 2002, *72,* 31–60.

DiMaggio, P., and Mohr, J. "Cultural Capital, Educational Attainment, and Marital Selection." *American Journal of Sociology,* 1985, *90,* 1231–1261.

Freeman, K. "Increasing African Americans' Participation in Higher Education: African American High School Students' Perspectives." *Journal of Higher Education,* 1997, *68,* 523–550.

Gladieux, L. E., and Swail, W. S. "Financial Aid Is Not Enough: Improving the Odds of College Success." In J. E. King (ed.), *Financing a College Education: How It Works, How It's Changing.* Washington, D.C.: Ace/Oryx Press, 1999.

Hearn, J. C. "Academic and Nonacademic Influences on the College Destinations of 1980 High School Graduates." *Sociology of Education,* 1991, *64,* 158–171.

Heller, D. E. "Student Price Response in Higher Education: An Update to Leslie and Brinkman." *Journal of Higher Education,* 1997, *68,* 624–659.

Heller, D. E. "The Effects of Tuition and State Financial Aid on Public College Enrollment." *Review of Higher Education,* 1999, *23,* 65–89.

Hossler, D., Schmit, J., and Vesper, N. *Going to College: How Social, Economic, and Educational Factors Influence the Decisions Students Make.* Baltimore: Johns Hopkins University Press, 1999.

Hurtado, S., Inkelas, K. K., Briggs, C., and Rhee, B. S. "Differences in College Access and Choice Among Racial/Ethnic Groups: Identifying Continuing Barriers." *Research in Higher Education,* 1997, *38*(1), 43–75.

Jackson, G. A. "Financial Aid, College Entry, and Affirmative Action." *American Journal of Education,* Aug. 1990, 523–550.

Kane, J., and Spizman, L. M. "Race, Financial Aid Awards, and College Attendance: Parents and Geography Matter." *American Journal of Economics and Sociology,* 1994, *53*(1), 73–97.

Kane, T. *The Price of Admission: Rethinking How Americans Pay for College.* Washington, D.C.: Brookings Institution, 1999.

Lamont, M., and Lareau, A. "Cultural Capital: Allusions, Gaps, and Glissandos in Recent Theoretical Developments." *Sociological Theory,* 1988, *6,* 153–168.

Leslie, L. L., and Brinkman, P. T. *The Economic Value of Higher Education.* Phoenix: American Council on Education and Oryx Press, 1988.

Lin, N. *Social Capital: A Theory of Social Structure and Action.* New York: Cambridge University Press, 2001.

Manski, C. F., and Wise, D. A. *College Choice in America.* Cambridge, Mass.: Harvard University Press, 1983.

McDonough, P. M. *Choosing Colleges: How Social Class and Schools Structure Opportunity.* Albany: State University of New York Press, 1997.

McDonough, P. M. "Counseling and College Counseling in America's High Schools." In D. A. Hawkins and J. Lautz (eds.), *State of College Admission* (pp. 107–121). Washington, D.C.: National Association for College Admission Counseling, 2005.

McPherson, M. A. "How Can We Tell If Financial Aid Is Working?" In M. S. McPherson, M. O. Shapiro, and G. C. Winston (eds.), *Paying the Piper: Productivity, Incentives, and Financing in U.S. Higher Education.* Ann Arbor: University of Michigan Press, 1993.

Monks, J. "The Returns to Individual and College Characteristics." *Economics of Education Review,* 2000, *19,* 279–289.

Myers, D., Olsen, R., Seftor, N., Young, J., and Tuttle, C. *The Impacts of Regular Upward Bound: The Results from the Third Follow-Up Data Collection.* Washington, D.C.: U.S. Department of Education, Office of the Undersecretary, Policy and Program Studies Service, 2004.

Paulsen, M. B., and St. John, E. P. "Social Class and College Costs: Examining the Financial Nexus Between College Choice and Persistence." *Journal of Higher Education,* 2002, *73,* 189–236.

Perna, L. W. "Differences in the Decision to Enroll in College Among African Americans, Hispanics, and Whites." *Journal of Higher Education,* 2000, *71,* 117–141.

Perna, L. W. "The Private Benefits of Higher Education: An Examination of the Earnings Premium." *Research in Higher Education,* 2003, *44,* 451–472.

Perna, L. W. "Understanding the Decision to Enroll in Graduate School: Sex and Racial/Ethnic Group Differences." *Journal of Higher Education,* 2004, *75,* 487–527.

Perna, L. W. "Studying College Choice: A Proposed Conceptual Model." In J. C. Smart (ed.), *Higher Education: Handbook of Theory and Research,* vol. 21 (pp. 99–157). New York: Springer, 2006.

Perna, L. W., and Titus, M. "The Relationship Between Parental Involvement as Social Capital and College Enrollment: An Examination of Racial/Ethnic Group Differences." *Journal of Higher Education,* 2005, *76,* 485–518.

Sewell, W. H., Hauser, R. M., and Wolf, W. C. "Sex, Schooling, and Occupational Status." *American Journal of Sociology,* 1986, *86,* 551–583.

St. John, E. P. "What Really Influences Minority Attendance? Sequential Analyses of the 'High School and Beyond' Sophomore Cohort." *Research in Higher Education,* 1991, *32,* 141–158.

St. John, E. P., and Asker, E. H. "The Role of Finances in Student Choice: A Review of Theory and Research." In M. B. Paulsen and J. C. Smart (eds.), *The Finance of Higher Education: Theory, Research, Policy, and Practice* (pp. 419–438). New York: Agathon Press, 2001.

St. John, E. P., and Noell, J. "The Effects of Student Financial Aid on Access to Higher Education: An Analysis of Progress with Special Consideration of Minority Enrollments." *Research in Higher Education,* 1989, *30,* 563–581.

Swail, W. S., and Perna, L. W. "Pre-College Outreach and Early Intervention Programs: A National Imperative." In W. G. Tierney and L. S. Hagedorn (eds.), *Increasing Access to College: Extending the Possibilities for All Students* (pp. 15–34). Albany: State University of New York Press, 2002.

Tierney, W. G. "Parents and Families in Precollege Preparation: The Lack of Connection Between Research and Practice." *Educational Policy,* 2002, *16,* 588–606.

Tierney, W. G., and Auerbach, S. "Toward Developing an Untapped Resource: The Role of Families in College Preparation." In W. G. Tierney (ed.), *Nine Propositions Relating to the Effectiveness of Early Intervention Programs.* Albany: State University of New York Press, 2005.

U.S. Census Bureau. *Statistical Abstract of the United States: 2001.* Washington, D.C.: Author, 2001.

U.S. Department of Education. *Base Year to Fourth Follow-Up Data File User's Manual: National Educational Longitudinal Study of 1988.* NCES 2002–323. Washington, D.C.: Office of Educational Research and Improvement, 2002a.

U.S. Department of Education. *Digest of Education Statistics, 2001.* NCES 2002–130. Washington, D.C.: National Center for Education Statistics, 2002b.

U.S. Department of Education. *Condition of Education, 2003*. Washington, D.C.: National Center for Education Statistics, 2003.

U.S. Department of Education. *Digest of Education Statistics, 2005*. NCES 2006–030. Washington, D.C.: National Center for Education Statistics, 2006.

U.S. Department of Labor, Bureau of Labor Statistics. *Occupational Outlook Handbook, 2002–03*. Washington, D.C.: U.S. Department of Labor, 2002.

U.S. Department of Labor, Bureau of Labor Statistics. *Tomorrow's Jobs*. Washington, D.C.: U.S. Department of Labor, 2003. http://www.bls.gov/oco/oco2003.htm. Accessed Oct. 3, 2006.

LAURA W. PERNA is associate professor of higher education at The University of Pennsylvania.

6

Employing a critical-empirical approach to the study of college access, the author explores the role of policy researchers in seeking educational equity.

Finding Social Justice in Education Policy: Rethinking Theory and Approaches in Policy Research

Edward P. St. John

The primacy of the scientific method in education research should be a source of concern among educators and policy researchers who focus on social justice in education. The U.S. Department of Education has adopted a narrow view of scientific research and experimental design (for example, the No Child Left Behind Act of 2001), an approach to framing research that constrains critical analyses of public policy. Further, the recent release of the Spellings Commission's report on higher education (U.S. Department of Education, 2006) illustrates the NCLB-type policies that higher education could soon be facing in the United States. In this chapter I propose an alternative approach to the use of quantitative research methods in educational policy research that is compatible with traditional quantitative methods but is also a more balanced approach.

The research on college access reported here was developed as part of a study of state financial indicators conducted for the Lumina Foundation on Education; this support is gratefully acknowledged. Glenda D. Musoba and Nate Daun-Barnett provided analyses that are summarized here; I appreciate their support and use "we" in the text as an acknowledgment of their collaboration. In addition, thanks to William Tierney and Frances Stage for providing thoughtful reviews of an earlier version of this chapter. The opinions expressed here are the author's and do not reflect official policies or positions of the Lumina Foundation.

Over the past two decades, I have been engaged in studies of educational policy issues that relate to equal opportunity and desegregation of higher education (for example, St. John, 1981). In recent years I have become concerned about the lack of authentic commitment to equal opportunity in official policy literature—material put out by the U.S. Department of Education and other federal agencies and lobbying organizations—that focuses on academic preparation for college (for example, Choy, 2001, 2002; Berkner and Chavez, 1997; Horn, 1997; Pelavin and Kane, 1988, 1990). Although the new concerns about preparation are no doubt critical, we should not lose sight of the goal of promoting equal opportunity in educational policy. It is therefore important to consider equity indicators along with preparation—often measured by achievement indicators—when examining the effects of reform strategies.

This chapter explores the role of policy researchers in the process of seeking justice in education policy. First, I present the critical-empirical approach that has guided this and other recent policy studies, and compare this approach to the scientific approach advocated in educational research. Second, I summarize the social justice framework that I developed in my recent book, *Refinancing the College Dream* (St. John, 2003), using this approach. I then summarize a case study of the influence of education policy on access to higher education using the new framework. Finally, I reflect on the case study in relation to the two approaches and conclude with some guidance for other researchers.

The Critical-Empirical Approach

In my early career I worked in government agencies and in consulting firms that conducted research on educational policy issues. My research focused on student aid (for example, St. John and Byce, 1982; St. John and Robinson, 1985) and the impact of student aid on student access and persistence (St. John and Masten, 1990; St. John and Noell, 1987, 1989), but it was difficult to address equal opportunity in these official roles. Instead, we were encouraged to release our findings only when they supported the policies advocated by the agencies we worked for or that funded our research. After an eight-year absence, I returned to academe in 1989 so I could begin to explore social equity issues more explicitly and purposefully.

One of my goals has been to develop an approach to framing policy research that allows me to test divergent claims, rather than being constrained by narrowly defined arguments devised by politicians and senior public officials who work for them. Influenced by Habermas's critical approach to social theory (Habermas, 1984), I began to work on defining a critical-empirical method (St. John, 1994, 1995, 1998). I have used this logical approach to explore a range of critical policy issues, often in collaborative projects (St. John and Elliott, 1994; St. John and Hossler, 1998; St. John, Loescher, and Bardzell, 2003; St. John and Miron, 2003; St. John and Paulsen, 2001;

NEW DIRECTIONS FOR INSTITUTIONAL RESEARCH • DOI: 10.1002/ir

ping Address
a Kee
CHARLES ST APT 2
)EN,MA 02148-6402
:d States

Item Price	Total
$44.00	$44.00
$29.00	$29.00

	$73.00
	$73.00
	$73.00
	$0.00

separately.

g.

www.amazon.com/ your-account

For detailed information about this and other orders, please visit Your Account. You can also print invoices, change your e-mail address and payment settings, alter your communication preferences, and much more - 24 hours a day - at http://www.amazon.com/your-account.

Returns Are Easy!

Visit http://www.amazon.com/returns to return any item - including gifts - in unopened or original condition within 30 days for a full refund (other restrictions apply). Please have your order ID ready.

Thanks for shopping at Amazon.com, and please come again!

little card
big smile™

amazongiftcards
www.amazon.com/giftcards

Type : V3

amazon.com

amazon.com 1850 Mercer Rd.
Lexington, KY 40511

Ayana Kee
255 CHARLES ST APT 2
MALDEN,MA 02148-6402
United States

Billing Address
Ayana Kee
255 CHARLES ST APT 2
MALDEN,MA 02148-6402
United States

Dpdbn9LbR/-2 of 2-/second/5927391 PXS

Your order of December 16, 2010 (Order ID 105-4595259-1697036

Qty.	Item
1	**Methods Matter: Improving Causal Inference in Educational and Social Science Research** Murnane, Richard J. --- Hardcover (** B-1 **) 0199753865
1	**Using Quantitative Data to Answer Critical Questions: New Directions for Institutional Research (J-B IR Single Issue Ins...** Stage, Frances K. --- Paperback (** B-1 **) 0787997781

Subtotal
Shipment Total
Paid via Visa
Balance due

We've sent this part of your order to ensure quicker service. The other items will shi

Have feedback on how we packaged your order? Tell us at www.amazon.com/packa

2/Dpdbn9LbR/-2 of 2-//PXS/second/5927391/1216-15:00/1216-11:39/aauterin Pad

St. John and Ridenour, 2001, 2002). This approach has given me freedom to produce a number of studies that pursue research agendas that emerged from critical reviews of large bodies of research on education problems. The critical-empirical approach is compared to the more traditional "scientific" method in Table 6.1.

The scientific method is commonly used in instrumental and strategic ways in education policy research. Habermas (1984) defined *strategic* action as being goal-oriented, or aimed at achieving a specific end. He argued that strategic action was *instrumental* if it was controlled by others and the actor was the instrument of an external policy or goal, or of the individual or institution promoting the goal. The scientific method as it is commonly used in education research is strategic, by either definition. The researcher reviews research, identifies a specific hypothesis, and designs a study that

Table 6.1. Comparison of the Scientific Approach and Critical-Empirical Approach

Dimension	Scientific Approach	Critical-Empirical Approach
Relation to theory and prior research	Review prior research and theory to develop a "hypothesis" that can be tested in a well-defined research study.	Review competing theories and diverse research pertaining to the policy problem. Identify different, possibly competing claims.
Accepted methods	Quantitative studies allow for accepting or rejecting hypothesis. Experimental designs, including natural experiments, are currently favored. Large-scale data collections and secondary data analyses are also frequently used.	Use methods appropriate for "testing" specific claims; often stated as questions rather than hypotheses. Methods depend on the nature of the theory and claim. May involve quantitative or qualitative research, critical reviews of research, or action experiments.
Role of research	Research is used to confirm and verify claims. Often offered as a "proof" of the theory, claim, or model.	Research is used to build understanding, develop theory, and inform action. Emphasis is on actionable knowledge.
Implications and limitations	Research often used for building rationales for reform. Research tends to be "self-sealing" and to overlook competing views.	Research examines competing views and can be used to open conversation. Research tends to be over looked in policy forums because of complexity.

can confirm the hypothesis (or can disconfirm the null hypothesis). Although in theory this method is intended to be neutral, it is easily manipulated by funding agencies or by researchers who have agendas of their own.

Education research is especially vulnerable to this type of instrumental manipulation when researchers set out to test their own beliefs in large-scale experiments or when policymakers fund analyses of extant data sources with the intent of generating research that supports their views on policy. In both cases, there is a heavy emphasis on proving the intended hypotheses, which are often tightly linked to policy goals and beliefs held by researchers and policymakers. Research becomes a mission with a goal of proving one's own beliefs and the effectiveness of the ideas, policies, and ideals advocated by the researchers and policymakers.

Critical research, including many qualitative studies, offers a counterview to the dominant perspective on education that is embedded in the new scientific model. In fact, research using critical social theory can illuminate the limitations of current policies by illuminating resulting inequalities. However, when critical studies work with a single theory, they too can fall into the trap of taking a self-sealing approach to confirming embedded beliefs. Thus, both quantitative and qualitative research can find it difficult to focus on building new common ground unless the claims of multiple positions are taken into account in policy research. In other words, critical research may stop short of informing the reconstruction of policy if it is not open to the possibility that mainstream claims might also be supported by evidence.

Communicative action, according to Habermas (1984), has the intent of *building understanding.* Consequently, the emphasis is on thinking critically about claims from diverse vantage points. Although the critique of social theory was the focus of Habermas's work, his approach can also be used in educational research. Using a philosophical approach that focuses on building understanding allows the researcher to develop studies that test competing claims. The key is to examine a range of claims that relate to a policy problem—claims that relate to our own intuitive position as well as claims that may not seem consonant with our beliefs.

Using the critical-empirical approach, I treat my own hunches as testable claims. It is possible to identify arguments others use as competing claims and design research that tests both types of claims. Often there is some truth—or validating information—related to each perspective. This method has given me the intellectual room and freedom to work with people whose views differ from my own, using research to build new understandings for people even if they hold different ideologies.

There are, of course, some limitations to using the critical-empirical approach. First and foremost, it is easy to deceive oneself by setting up alternative views as "straw men" to be knocked down. I have worked hard to avoid this trap, often reaching conclusions that are not consonant with the views I held when I began my research. For example, I have broadened my views on topics like using direct instruction and phonics in early reading (St. John,

Loescher, and Bardzell, 2003), privatization of higher education (St. John, 1994, 2003), and school choice (St. John and Ridenour, 2001, 2002). I remain committed to social justice, but I realize we need to open our minds to alternative positions if we are going to find new pathways through the puzzles we face in education policy.

Education Policy and Social Justice

Throughout my career, I have been concerned about how changes in educational policy, including public finance policies, influence educational opportunities and whether these policies move us closer to, or further from, the goal of ensuring equal opportunity. Recently I have used the critical-empirical approach as a review method to develop a framework for studying equal opportunity in education. I was interested in addressing gaps between theory in education, economics, sociology, and political science as they informed the policy debates about college access (St. John, 2003).

The model is situated in John Rawls's theory of justice (1971, 2001). This theory was used as a starting point both because it provided a moral basis for thinking about current education policy choices and because Rawls's principles provided a means of finding balance among competing interests in the education debates. He identifies three principles:

- Principle 1 relates to basic rights, which all individuals have in a democratic society. The rights to an education are nearly universally accepted (Nussbaum, 1999; Sen, 1999), and in the United States equal access to college should be a right for those who qualify academically.
- Principle 2 relates to equal opportunity, which argues that if there is an inequality it should favor the most disadvantaged. The historic emphases on equal opportunity in school desegregation and student aid are a few of many examples of this approach in education policy.
- The Just Savings Principle relates to cross-generation equity, which includes the use of taxation to support education. In the current context of majority concern about tax rates, it is important to balance taxpayer costs with concerns about equity and basic rights in education.

Using these principles helps illuminate the various interests in education, a step we need to take before we can find a better balance. Arguments about quality of education and academic preparation are generally framed in relation to achievement indicators—the types of courses students complete, their grades and test scores. These arguments are increasingly framed as basic rights (for example, Pennington, 2003). However, we also need ways to assess the equity effects of policies aimed at improving preparation, including their effects on high school graduation rates. Further, as new remedies are proposed, we need to consider costs of implementation because of the concern about taxes.

NEW DIRECTIONS FOR INSTITUTIONAL RESEARCH • DOI: 10.1002/ir

However, the theory of justice alone was not a sufficient basis for constructing a framework for educational research. Other areas of theory and research inform this framework:

- Economic theory on human capital and research on price response provide a basis for understanding how individuals respond to prices and subsidies.
- Social theory on attainment and reproduction provides a basis for understanding the tension between cultural reproduction and cross-generation uplift (for example, successive generations having higher levels of educational attainment), long a goal in the African American education tradition.
- Education research provides a way to articulate the linkages between specific education reforms and student outcomes.
- Policy theory and research help us understand that research can inform policy, even if rational policy models have seldom held up.

This framework identifies two sorts of outcomes of K–12 education: achievement outcomes (test scores and pass rates) and equity outcomes (retention and graduation rates). The achievement outcomes link to the "basic rights" claims being advanced by the new conservative reformers who advocated for the NCLB, which promotes testing and curriculum alignment across the United States. Although I do not agree that standardized tests adequately define the nature of basic education rights, as a researcher I can use test scores as measures of achievement, especially if I use them along with equity measures, such as the rates of students passing a grade level (in K–12 education) or students graduating from high school. Finding a balance between equity concerns and the newer claims about achievement and excellence is critical in education research. This sort of balance should be generally expected in policy research because of the ethos of NCLB, which includes an explicit claim about the success of all children and leaves room for using equity measures along with achievement measures in policy research.

My approach provides a way of linking the academic and financial claims about college access into a single framework. This conceptualization allows us to test competing views of college access. The three critical issues considered when using this framework to assess the impact of policies on outcomes are as follows:

- *Identify how policy links to outcomes and which variable should be controlled to assess these linkages.* Recent reviews of NCES studies (Becker, 2004; Heller, 2004) reveal a pattern of omitting crucial control variables and ignoring social theory when interpreting results.
- *Select indicators, or outcome measures, related to both basic rights and equity.* When assessing school reforms, consider measures related to achievement (basic right) and inclusiveness in attainment (retention rates, graduation rates, special education rates). In higher education, it is important to con-

sider the effects of policy interventions on outcomes for the majority and diverse groups.

• *Consider both types of indicators, along with the equity principle, when assessing the costs of alternatives.* The theories of efficiency and cost-benefit analysis borrowed from economics have been problematic because they have generally looked at one cost indicator in relation to one outcome indicator. The costs—the amounts taxpayers invest in education—must be weighed in relation to measures of both equity and quality.

An Example: State Policy and College Access

Over the past two years, I have worked with colleagues on studies that examine the impact of state education and finance policies on access-related outcomes. We created databases on states that included information for each state on population characteristics, education policies, finance policies, SAT scores, high school graduation rates, and college enrollment rates in the 1990s. We used a series of fixed-effects regressions to examine the influence of education policies.

Three analyses are presented as illustrations from the study. We constructed a database that included a record by state for each year between 1990 and 2005. Demographic characteristics of states were derived from census reports. This included the percentage of poverty in the state, the racial-ethnic composition of the state, and the percentage of the populations with bachelor's degrees. SAT participation rates and scores for each state each year were obtained from College Board reports. Information on state education policies was derived from reviews of national education databases. For each year, we examined the following for each state:

• The percentage of high schools offering Advanced Placement (AP) exams
• Whether the state had a policy on advanced, or honors, diplomas for high school graduates
• Whether the state had implemented math standards (most were consistent with recommendations of the National Council on Teaching Math)
• Whether the state required an examination to graduate high school
• Whether the state required three or more math courses for high school graduation (rather than only one or two math courses)
• Local discretion over setting the number of math courses for high school graduation (rather than only one or two math courses)
• K–12 expenditures per FTE

The analyses used fixed-effects regressions, a method that essentially controls for state effects. The analyses considered three outcomes: the average SAT score, the percent of the students in the cohort graduating high school, and the college enrollment rate for high school graduates. This approach was used to control for the role of state context. For one of the outcomes, college enrollment rates, data were available only for even years, so the number of cases was half the size of that for the other two analyses.

The first analysis (Table 6.2, column 1) examines the impact of state education policies on high school graduation rates. Poverty rates were not associated with high school graduation rates, nor were the percentages of minorities. However, the percentages of the population with bachelor's degrees were negatively associated with graduation rates. (Although there is evidence that parents' education is associated with educational attainment when individuals are studied [Choy, 2002], we should not expect that the percentage of the population with advanced education influences graduation rates, an attainment indicator.) Two types of policies had a positive association with graduation rates: high school exit examinations had a modest association and funding for K–12 schools had a strong association. Although this provides some support for advocates of testing (Finn, 1990; Paige, 2003), it does not support their argument that achievement is unrelated to school funding (see the following section). In addition, requiring more math courses for graduation was positively associated with high school graduation rates. The percentage of high schools in the state offering AP courses was positively associated with high school graduation rates, as it was with the other outcomes. Thus it is readily apparent that the different types of policies related to educational improvement have differential effects on high school graduation. Not all policies are equal, even when the same outcome is considered.

The second analysis (Table 6.2, column 2) examines the impact of state education policies on the state average SAT score, a widely used indicator of academic achievement, controlling for demographics and SAT participation rates in the state (from St. John, 2006). The poverty rate was negatively associated with SAT scores, the percentages of Hispanics and other minorities (mostly Asian) were positively associated with SAT scores, and the SAT participation rate was not significant when education reforms were considered. (In a prior step in the sequential logistic regression analysis, we found that SAT participation rates were positively associated with SAT scores; see St. John, 2006.) Controlling for these demographic characteristics, four of the education policies were positively associated with SAT scores: having implemented statewide standards in math, the percentage of high schools offering AP courses, providing more funding, and mandating three or more math courses for high school graduation. This analysis illustrates that many of the policies being implemented to improve educational outcomes are positively related to achievement, at least as measured by the SAT. The finding that educational funding is positively associated with test scores directly contradicts claims of neoconservatives to the contrary (for example, Finn, 1990; Paige, 2003).

However, these findings differ substantially from the findings on high school graduation rates. The same policies that had a positive association

Table 6.2. State Level Indicators of Academic Policies Predicting State Outcomes, 1990–2005

Independent Variables	High School Graduation Rate			SAT Average			College Continuation Rate		
	Coef.	St. Err.	Sig.	Coef.	St. Err.	Sig.	Coef.	St. Err.	Sig.
Percent below poverty	0.101	0.072		-50.645	28.847	**	-0.551	0.183	***
Percent African American	0.266	0.331		-64.340	148.072		-1.835	0.932	*
Percent Hispanic	-0.408	0.286		190.773	88.242	**	-0.646	0.531	
Percent other	0.134	0.184		-58.591	63.637	**	0.534	0.346	
K–12 expenditures ($1,000s)	-0.011	0.006	**	4.201	2.260		-0.019	0.000	
Percent adults with bachelor's	-0.153	0.075	*	131.524	29.670	***	0.279	0.185	
Enrollment of ninth-grade class (100,000s)	0.007	0.018		2.610	6.640		-0.077	0.014	*
High school exit exam required	-0.002	0.007		1.130	2.505		0.016	0.017	
State-adopted content standards	-0.023	0.003	***	10.660	1.536	***	-0.004	0.011	
Honors diploma available	-0.006	0.006		-2.372	2.100		-0.003	0.012	
Required to complete three or more math courses	-0.031	0.006	***	4.762	2.071	**	0.019	0.013	
Local district in control of math requirements	0.018	0.012		-6.069	4.409		0.052	0.025	**
SAT participation rate	0.000	0.000		-90.380	0.033	***	-0.213	0.162	
Percent of high schools with AP courses	0.078	0.043	***	15.990	9.252	*	0.136	0.059	**
Observations	491			585			248		
Groups	50			50			50		
F-statistic	33.69		***	40.7		***	10.7		***

Note: *** $p < 0.01$, ** $p < 0.05$, * $p < 0.1$.

with SAT scores also had a negative association with graduation rates, further indicating the contradictory nature of some of the education policies that are being widely implemented.

Although the findings on graduation rates indicated that policies had contradictory effects for the same outcome, the findings illustrate that the claims about policy being made by conservatives are not nearly as simple as they make them out to be.

The final analysis examines the impact of the same demographic characteristics and K–12 policies on college continuation rates (Table 6.2, column 3). As expected, poverty and the percent African American were negatively associated with college continuation rates.. However, the size of the cohort had a negative association with graduation rates, indicating that large states face some particularly complex issues. The percentage of high schools with AP courses was positively associated with college continuation rates, as it was for high school graduation and SAT scores. In addition, local control of high school graduation requirements, compared to requiring two math courses, had a positive association with continuation rates. Again, some imbalance in policy is evident: excellence policies (that is, standards and state-imposed requirements) do not necessarily encourage all students.

Looking across these three analyses it is evident that education reform is not as simple as assumed by NCLB advocates and the Spellings Commission (U.S. Department of Education, 2006), which promotes a similar ideology. Raising standards and increasing requirements have contradictory effects. Just because policies cause some students to take more advanced courses, it does not mean these policies help all children. These policies could apparently discourage some children from completing high school. At the very least, they induce dropout. This imbalance in K–12 policy is important because the espoused intention of NCLB is to "leave no child behind," which means to enable more children to graduate high school. The sad irony is that even though the new policies essentially restrict the percentage of children who graduate high school, they do not increase the percentage of high school graduates who go on to college. If one of the goals of school reform is to improve the preparation of high school graduates for college, then there is still more reason to question the current direction of K–12 reform.

Using the critical-empirical perspective to interpret these findings makes it possible to contribute to policy conversation without feeling compromised in my commitment to social equity. Studies like this one clearly illustrate that there are some ways that the new education policies contribute to social progress for diverse groups in American society. At the same time, these studies illustrate some of the serious limitations of the policy course on which we are now embarked. Although the new policies are aligned with improved achievement as measured by standardized tests, they also systematically leave more children behind. It is important to illuminate both outcomes if we are to maintain hope of constructing equitable policy pathways in the future.

These findings are especially important for higher education administrators and researchers given the emphasis on high school performance and accountability in the Spellings report (U.S. Department of Education, 2006). The report advocates heaping more requirements on high schools and imposing greater accountability in colleges. Their argument is based on studies of the high school class of 1992 and overlooked the changes in policy and student outcomes since that time, as is abundantly evident from the analyses reported here. These schemes have not worked well for K–12: buying into accountability schemes to get a few dollars more seems shortsighted. It is time for researchers and administrators in higher education and K–12 education to reflect openly and collectively.

Guidance for Researchers

It is difficult to find social justice in education policy these days. School reform is moving rapidly toward test-driven policies that have detrimental effects on equal opportunity. Also, the most substantial growth in state financial aid programs has been in merit aid (Heller and Rasmussen, 2001), a form of aid that is associated with higher high school dropout rates (St. John, 2006).

If we maintain open minds and use the results of critical-empirical studies, then we must acknowledge the strength of the excellence-driven reforms: they can improve achievement. Yet the goal of leaving no child behind gets more and more remote when these extreme policies dominate, a conclusion that is supported by the research evidence. At the very least, a better balance is needed in both education and public finance policies—equity considerations merit more attention.

Stepping back from these analyses to review the themes introduced at the outset of the chapter, it is apparent that it is possible to use balanced approaches to policy analysis that bring an emphasis on equal opportunity back into education policy research. To do this, I have found it necessary to contend with my own biases if I am to engage in the policy discourse without feeling personally compromised. Being critical *and* constructive makes it less difficult to be involved in policy conversations. There is always a need for external critics, but there is also a need for open-minded people at the policy tables.

The critical-empirical approach offers a way through the puzzle for critical scholars willing to engage in policy conversations. It offers the chance to examine arguments critically, without assuming a side on every specific issue. After all, the goal of equal opportunity supercedes any specific policy position or program feature because it is a guiding principle in moving toward better public policy in education and finance. The basic right to a quality education should also be a guiding value, but it should no longer be the dominant value in education policy.

Both of these values—equal opportunity and quality education—also need to be balanced with concern about taxpayer costs and returns on public investment. The current education and public finance policies encourage large numbers of children to drop out, a troublesome outcome for both conservatives and new liberals. (New liberal democrats have also supported excellence initiatives—such as standards on testing—since the 1980s.) A better economy depends on making better use of tax dollars to ensure equal opportunity for a quality education.

It is also crucial to deal with social conservatives' claims about efficiency. For decades, new conservative reforms have argued that equity costs too much (Finn, 1990). However, as the study summarized here reveals, the excellence initiatives are inefficient because they leave so many children behind.

References

Becker, W. E. "Omitted Variables and Sample Selection in Studies of College-Going Decisions." In E. P. St. John (ed.), *Readings on Equal Education. Vol. 19: Public Policy and College Access: Investigating the Federal and State Roles in Equalizing Postsecondary Opportunity* (pp. 65–86). New York: AMS Press, Inc., 2004.

Berkner, L., and Chavez, L. *Access to Higher Postsecondary Education for the 1992 High School Graduates.* NCES 98–105. Washington, D.C.: National Center for Education Statistics, 1997.

Choy, S. *Students Whose Parents Did Not Go to College: Postsecondary Access, Persistence, and Attainment.* Washington, D.C.: National Center for Education Statistics, 2001.

Choy, S. P. *Access & Persistence: Findings from 10 Years of Longitudinal Research on Students.* Washington, D.C.: American Council on Education, 2002.

Finn, C. E., Jr. "The Biggest Reform of All." *Phi-Delta-Kappan,* 1990, 71(8), 584–592.

Habermas, J. *The Theory of Communicative Action.* Vols. 1 and 2. Cambridge, England: Polity Press, 1984.

Heller, D. E. "NCES Research on College Participation: A Critical Analysis." In E. P. St. John (ed.), *Readings on Equal Education. Vol. 19: Public Policy and College Access: Investigating the Federal and State Roles in Equalizing Postsecondary Opportunity* (pp. 29–64). New York: AMS Press, Inc., 2004.

Heller, D. E, and Rasmussen, C. J. "Merit Scholarships and College Access: Evidence from Two States." Paper presented at the Civil Rights Project Forum on State Merit Aid Programs, College Access and Equity, Harvard University, Dec. 2001.

Horn, L. J. *Confronting the Odds: Students at Risk and the Pipeline to Higher Education.* NCES 98–094. Washington, D.C.: National Center for Education Statistics, 1997.

Nussbaum, M. C. *Sex and Social Justice.* Oxford, England: Oxford University Press, 1999.

Paige, R. "More Spending Is Not the Answer. Opposing View: Improving Quality of Schools Calls for High Standards, Accountability." *USA Today,* Jan. 10, 2003, p. 11A.

Pelavin, S. H., and Kane, M. B. *Minority Participation in Higher Education.* Washington, D.C.: Pelavin Associates, 1988.

Pelavin, S. H., and Kane, M. B. *Changing the Odds: Factors Increasing Access to College.* New York: College Board, 1990.

Pennington, H. "The Economic Imperative for 'Doubling the Numbers': Release of Research About the Nation's Need and Will to Improve Postsecondary Attainment." Paper presented at Double the Numbers: Postsecondary Attainment and Underrepresented Youth, Washington, D.C., Oct. 23, 2003.

Rawls, J. *A Theory of Justice.* Cambridge, Mass.: Belknap Press, 1971.

Rawls, J. *Justice as Fairness: A Restatement.* (E. Kelly, ed.) Cambridge, Mass.: Harvard University Press, 2001.

Sen, A. *Development as Freedom.* New York: Anchor, 1999.

St. John, E. P. *Public Policy and College Management: Title III of the Higher Education Act.* New York: Praeger Press, 1981.

St. John, E. P. *Prices, Productivity, and Investment: Assessing Financial Strategies in Higher Education.* ASHE/ERIC Higher Education Study. Washington, D.C.: George Washington University, 1994.

St. John, E. P. "Rethinking Tuition and Student Aid Strategies." In E. P. St. John (ed.), *Rethinking Tuition and Student Aid Strategies.* New Directions for Higher Education, no. 89. San Francisco: Jossey-Bass, 1995.

St. John, E. P. "Higher Education Desegregation in the Post-*Fordice* Legal Environment: An Historical Perspective." In R. E. Fossey (ed.), *Readings on Equal Education.* Vol. 15: *Race, the Courts, and Equal Education: The Limits of the Law* (pp. 101–122). New York: AMS Press, 1998.

St. John, E. P. *Refinancing the College Dream: Access, Equal Opportunity, and Justice for Taxpayers.* Baltimore: Johns Hopkins University Press, 2003.

St. John, E. P. *Education and the Public Interest: Education Reform, Public Finance, and Access to Higher Education.* New York: Springer, 2006.

St. John, E. P., and Byce, C. "The Changing Federal Role in Student Financial Aid." In M. Kramer (ed.), *Meeting Student Aid Needs in a Period of Retrenchment.* New Directions in Higher Education, no. 40. San Francisco: Jossey-Bass, 1982.

St. John, E. P., and Elliott, R. J. "Reframing Policy Research." In J. C. Smart (ed.), *Higher Education: Handbook of Theory and Research* (pp. 126–180). New York: Agathon Press, 1994.

St. John, E. P., and Hossler, D. "Higher Education Desegregation in the Post-*Fordice* Legal Environment: A Critical-Empirical Perspective." In R. Fossey (ed.), *Readings on Equal Education.* Vol. 15: *Race, the Courts, and Equal Education: The Limits of the Law* (pp. 123–156). New York: AMS Press, 1998.

St. John, E. P., Loescher, S. A., and Bardzell, J. S. *Improving Reading and Literacy in Grades 1-5: A Resource Guide to Research-Based Programs.* Thousand Oaks, CA: Corwin, 2003.

St. John, E. P., and Masten, C. L. "Return on the Federal Investment in Student Financial Aid: An Assessment of the High School Class of 1972." *Journal of Student Financial Aid,* 1990, *20*(3), 4–23.

St. John, E. P., and Miron, L. F. (eds.). *Reinterpreting Urban School Reform: Have Urban Schools Failed, or Has the Reform Movement Failed Urban Schools?* (pp. 279-298). Albany: State University of New York Press, 2003.

St. John, E. P., and Noell, J. "Student Loans and Higher Education Opportunities: Evidence on Access, Persistence, and Choice of Major." Fourth annual NASSGP/NCHELP Research Network Conference. St. Louis, July 1987.

St. John, E. P., and Noell, J. "The Impact of Financial Aid on Access: An Analysis of Progress with Special Consideration of Minority Access." *Research in Higher Education,* 1989, *30*(6), 563–582.

St. John, E. P., and Paulsen, M. B. "The Finance of Higher Education: Implications for Theory, Research, Policy, and Practice." In M. B. Paulsen and J. C. Smart (eds.), *The Finance of Higher Education: Theory, Research, Policy, & Practice.* New York: Agathon Press, 2001.

St. John, E. P., and Ridenour, C. "Market Forces and Strategic Adaptation: The Influence of Private Scholarships on Planning in Urban School Systems." *Urban Review,* 2001, *33*, 269–290.

St. John, E. P., and Ridenour, C. S. "School Leadership in a Market Setting: The Influence of Private Scholarships on Education Leadership in Urban Schools." *Leadership and Policy in Schools,* 2002, *1*(4), 317–344.

St. John, E. P., and Robinson, L. A. "Redesign of the Delivery Systems for Federal Student Aid Programs." *Cause/Effect,* 1985, 8(5), 46–48.
U.S. Department of Education. *A Test of Leadership: Changing the Future of U.S. Higher Education.* Washington, D.C.: Author, 2006.

EDWARD P. ST. JOHN is the Algo D. Henderson Collegiate Professor of Education at the University of Michigan's Center for the Study of Higher and Postsecondary Education.

NEW DIRECTIONS FOR INSTITUTIONAL RESEARCH • DOI: 10.1002/ir

7

The author introduces her critical and feminist perspective, elaborates on her critical approach, and discusses how this influenced the development of her research questions, methodology, data analysis, interpretation, and presentation of findings.

Women's Paths in Science: A Critical Feminist Analysis

Jillian Kinzie

> To adopt a woman's perspective means to see things one did not see before and also to see the familiar rather differently.
> —Joyce McCarl Nielsen

Like many young girls growing up in the early 1970s, I played the popular Selchow & Righter board game "What Shall I Be?" that matched girls' traits with possible careers. I imagined myself in the glamorous career roles of stewardess, nurse, or fashion designer. Pilot, scientist, and doctor were not among the possible career options in this game geared toward girls. Yet, prior to age eight, I harbored a desire to be a doctor. One of my favorite toys was a little red doctor bag filled with a play stethoscope, syringe, otoscope, and doctor's spectacles. I was always looking for volunteer patients. I suspect my early abandonment of my red doctor bag for the allure of a stewardess uniform was a harbinger of my departure from science in college.

My childhood reflections, a personally discouraging experience in college science, and my work as an academic advisor, which revealed qualitatively different experiences among men and women students in college science, influenced my decision to pursue a research agenda on women in science. I wondered about the contemporary situation for women in science. As a feminist, I questioned the popular message that girls and women can be whatever they want if they work hard enough and want it badly

NEW DIRECTIONS FOR INSTITUTIONAL RESEARCH, no. 133, Spring 2007 © Wiley Periodicals, Inc.
Published online in Wiley InterScience (www.interscience.wiley.com) • DOI: 10.1002/ir.206

enough (Ad Council, 2002; Kubanek and Waller, 1995). Are the doors to a major in science that were once closed to women now open? Had career opportunities expanded so that more women were entering and persisting in traditionally male-dominated fields? If women's participation rates remain unchanged, what is the source of the problem? Had the expansion of educational equity and promise of women's liberation reduced the hurdles and off-ramps for women on the science career track?

I offer this introduction to document how I arrived at the topic of my research and to hint at the epistemological and methodological assumptions that frame my inquiry. When I began conducting educational research I subscribed to a perspective that was influenced by my own experience and informed by a postpositivist epistemology that social reality is constructed and is created differently by individuals. According to Lincoln and Guba (1985), multiple social realities cannot be studied by the typical analytic methods of positivist research because they must be studied holistically. Although this view places me squarely in a qualitative paradigm, I value the descriptive and explanatory power of quantitative research and believe that both qualitative and quantitative approaches help educational researchers make important discoveries. Consequently, my approach to educational inquiry is grounded in the values of social construction, equity, and transformation traditionally associated with critical and feminist theory.

Though my primary commitment is to the feminist research tradition, I became increasingly interested in critical theory as an approach that furthered the emancipatory aims of feminism. Nielsen (1990) associates the feminist approach to research with the philosophy of critical theory because both reject the claim that any position can be neutral or disinterested and adopt a commitment to liberating people from constricting ideologies. In addition, the perspectives share a belief that knowledge is socially constructed and interpreted.

In this chapter, I introduce a research project that I conducted from a critical and feminist perspective as a means to illustrate these approaches. I then elaborate on my critical approach and discuss how this influenced the development of my research questions, data analysis and interpretation, and presentation of findings.

Women's Pathways to Science and Mathematics

My research project was undertaken from a critical and feminist methodological framework and employed a nationally representative data set to follow a cohort of female students from eighth grade through postsecondary education. The aim was to reveal differences among the students based on the pathways they pursued in science and mathematics education. By focusing on female student responses regarding their intended major at two critical junctures in their academic career—senior year in high school and two years into postsecondary education—I defined four distinct pathways pursued by women related to science and mathematics, including "Joiners," who enter the math-science pipeline after high school. Results contradict some work on the pipeline where women are described as only leaving. Following a description of the research, I discuss the features that make this quantitative study critical.

The underrepresentation of girls and women in science has been a long-standing concern of educators and policymakers (Davis and Associates, 1996; Hanson, 1996; Oakes, 1990; Seymour, 2001; Thom, 2001). Evidence of a gender gap emerges as early as age nine and is cumulative as girls move through school. The absence of advanced math and science courses on women's high school transcripts contributes to women arriving at college with low interest levels in math and science and lacking the prerequisites for many college programs, thereby limiting their choice of major (Davis and Associates, 1996; Seymour, 2001). However, even women who come to college with necessary prerequisites and an interest in science abandon their plans early on for various reasons (Seymour, 2001).

Although women's enrollment in college has increased so that they are now the majority, the widest gender gap remains in their enrollment in science, technology, engineering, and mathematics (STEM) programs (National Center for Education Statistics [NCES], 2000; Thom, 2001). In fact, the NCES report indicates that women's enrollment rates in postsecondary science and engineering programs are less than half of men's, 7.6 percent and 20.4 percent, respectively.

At the postsecondary level, women earned only 34 percent of the total science, mathematics, and engineering bachelor's degrees conferred in 1995–96 (National Center for Education Statistics, 2000). The 1997 National Science Foundation report *Women and Science* indicated that despite a surge in the proportion of women majoring in science in the 1970s and early 1980s, this number has not budged since the mid-1980s (Selingo, 1998).

More recent national data on degree attainment indicate a slight increase for women in several science areas, but it is noteworthy that in 2003–04 women accounted for only 25 percent of the computer information and science bachelor degree recipients and 19 percent of the engineering and engineering technology degree recipients (National Center for Education Statistics, 2006). Moreover, in the mid-1980s, the Higher Education Research Institute drew attention to the decline in the number of new college students choosing to enter STEM majors as well as 40 percent declines in the persistence rates of science majors, particularly women, between the first and senior year (Astin, Tsui, and Avalos, 1996). The research group also found wide disparities between the percentages of incoming women's and men's declarations of science majors, 10 and 25 percent, respectively (Sax, Astin, Korn, and Mahoney, 1998). Finally, a recent analysis of trends in student persistence and attainment in science and engineering published by the National Council for Research on Women (Thom, 2001) suggested that entering a postsecondary institution does not guarantee success for underrepresented and minority female students because they

NEW DIRECTIONS FOR INSTITUTIONAL RESEARCH • DOI: 10.1002/ir

are confronted with more challenges of a psychocultural nature than other students. Despite efforts to dismantle gender stereotyping and to make the climate in science and math more hospitable to girls and women, and to expand women's life roles to consider careers in science, women abandon their plans to study science and mathematics at disproportionate rates.

Research on the factors that influence women's choice of science, mathematics, and engineering majors suggests multiple influences, including traditional predictors of achievement, aptitude, course-taking patterns, attitudes toward science and mathematics, and additional factors such as self-concept, math beliefs, and student's math and science behaviors (Huang, Taddese, and Walter, 2000; Maple and Stage, 1991; Seymour, 2001). Women's beliefs about their academic abilities and levels of self-efficacy have been shown to influence their choice of college major. Notably, academic aptitude (as measured by the SAT) has been shown to account for only some of the variance in the gendered nature of college major choice. Students' value systems and their gender role orientation were found to be significant predictors of choice of college major. It is clear that women's choice of STEM major is not just a matter of academic ability. Rather, there appears to be a complex constellation of factors that constrain women's participation in science and mathematics.

The process of choosing a major begins well before college (Maple and Stage, 1991). Indeed, the paucity of women in science majors is attributable to factors affecting girls and women during the elementary and secondary school years (Oakes, 1990; Hanson, 1996). Critical junctures in middle school, sophomore and senior years of high school, and the transition from high school to college are entry and exit points for girls and women in science. However, most of the research has studied the vast migration out of the science talent pool. For example, Seymour and Hewitt (1997) documented the problem of high school graduates who are prepared for and interested in science but leave the science and math track by switching to other majors.

Past studies have provided a foundation for understanding women's participation in STEM education. However, a rise in women choosing and succeeding in science and mathematics majors is dependent on increasing the number of girls and women in the science talent pool. Enhancing our understanding of the characteristics of girls and women who choose STEM majors and persist in them versus those who leave and those who choose other majors is important. Further, understanding the critical points when these differences emerge can lead to the reduction of sexist structures and the creation of educational practices and policies that are more empowering for women and effective at increasing their participation in science and mathematics.

Research Methodology

Although this study furthers existing efforts to understand inequities in women's participation, my study differs in a few ways. First, gender is central to it. For example, I began with an assumption of gender difference and as a result did not reproduce the typical comparison between women and men. Second, I further investigated variability among girls and women and tried to avoid universalizing women's experience. Third, I sought to identify the practices and structures that disadvantage women.

Employing data from the National Educational Longitudinal Study (NELS:88), I followed a cohort (N = 3,148) of female students from eighth grade through postsecondary education (Kinzie, 1999). By focusing on female student responses regarding intended major at two critical junctures in their academic career—senior year in high school and two years into postsecondary education—I revealed differences between these students based on the pathways they pursued and defined four distinct pathways pursued by women related to science and mathematics. Women were classified into one of the following four groups: (1) "Nevers," or women who in twelfth grade were not interested in pursuing a science degree and did not declare a STEM major in college; (2) "Departers," or women who in twelfth grade declared an interest in science and then selected a non-STEM major in college; (3) "Joiners," or women who in twelfth grade did not declare an interest in science but selected a STEM college major; and finally (4) "Persisters," or women who in twelfth grade declared an interest in science and who later selected a STEM major in college. I used discriminant analysis to identify variables that were the best predictors of women's educational choice. Predictor variables included academic achievement in mathematics, self-concept, educational aspirations, science grades, academic behaviors related to math and science courses, course-taking patterns, science and math attitudes and beliefs, and socioeconomic status and race or ethnicity (a total of twenty-three measures), at three crucial points in their educational path—eighth grade, tenth grade, and twelfth grade. By defining four distinct pathways, I moved beyond the typical, straightforward dichotomous outcome of women as leaving or staying in the mathematics and science talent pool.

Results and Interpretation

Using discriminant function analysis, women students' paths in science and math education can be predicted from a variety of traditional psychological, behavioral, and achievement-related variables at three points in their educational careers. Findings confirm that as early as eighth grade, distinctions can be made between girls and women with regard to the pathways they pursue. Math achievement functions as the "critical filter" to admission to STEM majors. The strength of this variable, significant in the eighth- and tenth-grade models, suggests that greater attention needs to be placed on improving girls' math achievement levels in adolescence. Low math achievement levels in eighth grade could also play a role in further diminishing women's interest in math, thereby reducing the number and level of math courses taken in high school, resulting in lower numbers of women being prepared to pursue math and science in college. Science grades also act as a filter through which few women pass. The confluence of science grades and math achievement demonstrates that girls and women simultaneously receive signals about their participation in science and math education from two important sources. In addition, Persisters were distinguished in eighth grade by their more positive beliefs about science and math. This suggests the power that beliefs have to confirm and constrain women's educational expectations. Considered interdependently, math achievement, science grades, and beliefs about self in science and math exerted a strong influence on choice of major.

The general measure of self-concept—a person's self-perceptions formed through experience with and interpretations of one's environment—used in this study was a strong predictor for Departers, women who migrated from their plans to major in college science. These women possessed a more positive self-concept than other groups. This finding may seem counterintuitive, but given the lack of distinction offered in such an omnibus measure, it is not surprising. However, an examination of trends in this indicator over time—in eighth, tenth, and twelfth grade—reveals that only the self-concept scores of girls in the Persisters group increased. The discrepancies surrounding this variable suggest the importance of examining field-specific measures of self-concept, particularly with women in underrepresented fields.

In addition to math achievement and science grades, in tenth grade educational aspiration was a significant predictor in distinguishing Persisters from Nevers. Although the aspirations of Persisters rose steadily through their educational path, for Nevers it dropped significantly. This finding emphasizes the importance of early expectations for high levels of education for women in nontraditional fields. Girls and women who develop early expectations for high levels of educational attainment are more likely to make earlier declarations of their interest in science and math and to persist in science education in college. In twelfth grade, Persisters are unequivocally defined from the other groups by their participation in more upper-level math courses in high school, and science and math effort, estimated by the time they spent on science and math homework.

The group identified as Joiners—women who do not declare an interest in science and math fields early in high school and then in college declare a science major—is an important group to understand. First, because women in this group did not identify their interest in science and math early in high school, they may have been overlooked with regard to student services and educational interventions designed to support girls and women, such as special math and science precollege programs, or academic advising regarding appropriate math and science high school courses. Second, socioeconomic status defined students in this group, indicating that Joiners might lack some of the advantages, for example, of having educational objects such as calculators, computers, and encyclopedias in the home, resources typically associated with educational success. Third, in tenth grade these women possessed attitudes toward math and science that may be viewed as negative, such as not working hard in science or math and infrequently reviewing math and science work. These views could be the result of feeling unchallenged by high school courses. However, given that in twelfth grade Joiners had the lowest grade point average in math courses, taken together these findings could be strong indicators for insufficient preparation for college science courses.

Either way, knowing that poor attitudes and low grades in math courses characterize women in the Joiners group, this raised questions about the adequacy of women's preparation for college science courses. Moreover, it is important to attend to the ways in which these women differ from those in the Persisters group, because they all may end up in the same introductory chemistry course in college. Regardless, the promotion of positive beliefs about self and science and math, in particular, where girls look forward to math class and feel that their questions are valued in the science classroom, are essential to increasing the participation rates of women in science and math.

It is unlikely that a panacea will be found to make science and mathematics attractive to all girls and women. However, increasing the number of women who persist in science from among the three groups of women who, at minimum, indicate some inclination toward science and math—Persisters, Joiners, and Departers—seems the most effective approach to improving the participation of women in STEM fields. In addition, it is especially important to study Joiners and Departers as borderline participants in the field. Moreover, it is important to develop a deeper understanding of the full constellation of obstacles that constrain women's decisions to pursue science education. The more we understand the factors that distinguish women and the educational pathways they pursue, the better equipped we will be to eliminate oppressive structures and design educational interventions to increase the number of women who choose and remain in STEM majors.

Critical and Feminist Commitments

In this section I review why I chose this topic, my methodological commitment, and where the research has taken me.

Choice of Topic and Research Questions. As detailed in the opening paragraphs of this chapter, my personal experiences as a student and academic advisor, and my explicit interest in doing educational research that addresses gender inequities, brought me to the subject of my inquiry. This perspective is in accordance with Reinharz's (1992) contention that "feminist researchers frequently start with an issue that bothers them personally and then use everything they can get a hold of to study it" (p. 259). In addition, critical theory rejects the idea that neutrality is a necessary condition of inquiry. As a result, the starting point for my research was subjective, emerging from my personal experiences in science and with undergraduate women in science. My interest was advanced by my growing concern about addressing the gender gap in science.

NEW DIRECTIONS FOR INSTITUTIONAL RESEARCH • DOI: 10.1002/ir

My personal concern about women's underrepresentation in science prompted me to frame this study as an examination of inequities. For example, I wanted to identify the hurdles and off-ramps for women on the science career track and what effect they had on women's educational choices. Moreover, I viewed the constraints on women's educational choices and their resulting limits on women's future economic opportunities as social and economic injustices that must be eradicated. Feminist and critical frameworks advocate that such injustices be exposed so they can be dismantled.

Feminism also influenced my decision that my research question must originate from the perspective of women. Researchers working in the critical tradition investigate social problems and phenomena with groups whose voices have been silenced by the dominant power structure. In addition, because critical and feminist frameworks take into account how gender shapes our lives, institutions, organizations, and the distribution of power and privilege (Lather, 1991), gender was the basic analytic category in this study. Other mediating forces including race or ethnicity, class, and sexual orientation were also integrated into this critical work.

Although extant research formed the foundation of my examination of women's educational paths, it is important to distinguish where my research questions departed from traditional approaches. Unlike the research questions of existing studies on the math and science pipeline, which focused on comparing a collection of characteristics and experiences between males and females in terms of their participation in math and science education, I elected to compare differences among women alone. Earlier research considered traditional variables including standardized test scores and course-taking behaviors and assumed that the factors that were important to the experiences of both women and men were the same. In contrast, my critical framework presumed that traditional predictors are mediated by gender and race or ethnicity and would have differential impacts among women. Furthermore, research that included additional background variables such as the mother's and father's educational levels, socioeconomic status, type of high school attended, and measures of self-concept and beliefs about science and mathematics to examine gender differences were helpful to my work because they provided a richer context for my examination of women students.

The approaches and research questions in extant research influenced my work by exposing biases in the body of research. As a result, I chose to focus on women, not in comparison to men, and expanded my research questions to examine their unique situation. Further, I did not enter this work from a neutral, objective standpoint. Instead, I entered this work from a personal standpoint and believed in the importance of identifying barriers to women's participation in math and science education in order to eliminate oppressive structures and create conditions that empower girls and women.

Methodological Commitments. According to Harding (1987), methodology is the theory of knowledge and interpretive framework that guides research. My methodological commitments are rooted in feminist and critical theory. These approaches to inquiry share a commitment to investigate power relationships, examine lived experiences, expose oppression, and address inequalities. To explore this approach to educational research, and as Nielsen (1990) suggests, to "see the familiar differently," I adopted different vantage points, considered the aims of my research, and tried on alternative methodological lenses to view my questions.

As an example of seeing the familiar differently, I reconsidered more than thirty years of national statistics on women's participation in science education. These statistics were gathered to monitor success in achieving parity in the science talent pool. Increases in the percentage of girls completing high school science and math courses, rises in the number of women entering undergraduate and graduate programs, and the diversification of the science workforce are considered indicators of expanded opportunities for women. However, my concern with these statistics is that although they demonstrate progress, they mislead us into thinking that equity in science is simply a matter of adding women into the science talent pool. In addition, these measures are produced in what Lather (1992) identified as a paradigm of prediction, rather than a paradigm of disclosure and advocacy. Finally, these measures add little to our understanding of the complexities of the situation and suggest that if there is a goal to be attained, it is merely to achieve parity. Feminist and critical frameworks led me to question this belief in equity based on numerical increases, and eventual parity, and prompted me to consider how girls' and women's lives, and the situation for women in science, are viewed through feminism, and are mediated by gender and shaped by systems of inequity such as classism, racism, and sexism.

Choice of Method. Feminist research approaches advocate a range of methods in quantitative inquiry (Reinharz, 1992). For example, proponents of feminist empiricism advocate eliminating gender biases in research but support the use of conventional scientific methods, whereas others argue that the parameters of quantitative research are antithetical to feminist principles. Critical theory is perhaps even more stringently opposed to the use of quantitative research. However, in this case, a study conducted from a critical and feminist perspective views women's experiences as source and subject of research.

My decision to conduct research on an existing national database limited my use of critical and feminist methods. For example, I was limited to the traditional variables in the data set. A critical study would have included additional cultural and contextual variables and employed multiple methods. Reinharz (1992) advocates "dual vision," meaning using more than one method, as an approach frequently used by feminist researchers. In addition, without important cultural variables, I was limited in my ability to envision the kinds of approaches that remove barriers to women and increase their participation in science and mathematics education.

A benefit of using a large national data set is the ability to disaggregate. As a result, I had a large enough sample to focus solely on women students.

NEW DIRECTIONS FOR INSTITUTIONAL RESEARCH • DOI: 10.1002/ir

Yoder and Kahn (1993) argued that because the world is not the same for men and women, it is important to focus on women alone and to consider their experience in a social context. They caution researchers against relying on a comparative research framework because it can reinforce and perpetuate male as normative. To produce an interpretation more representative of women's lives, it is important to situate research from the vantage point of women and to examine race and class issues that prevent universalizing to women in general and acknowledge multiple subjectivities.

The feminist and critical traditions provide an alternative to the dominant theories and methods and aim to reveal gender biases and produce a more complete account of the world. As a result, I have attempted to see the world through women's eyes, and to reveal a more complete explanation of their participation in science and mathematics. By conducting quantitative research from a critical feminist perspective, I was able to examine the complexities of women's experiences and to take this into account in a discussion of recommendations.

Interpretation of Results and Implications. Conventional approaches to research on women in mathematics and science resulted in explanations of the differential experiences of males and females as attributable to individual differences rather than to the consequences of a male-ordered world (Scott, 1988), and to deficiencies in girls' and women's background in math and science. For example, girls' limited math and science course-taking in middle and high school and their low scores on standardized math and science achievement tests were identified as deficiencies in their preparation and aptitude. In contrast to this deficit model, a critical and feminist interpretation of this finding would expose the difference as an injustice and advocate transformations in the sexist structure.

Critical theory also lends a different interpretation of the classic characterization of women being filtered out of the sciences from middle school through postsecondary education. Instead of viewing this as only about women's departure, critical theory advocates a more comprehensive examination of women's participation by taking into account how and at what point women depart, and where they might enter or reenter the pipeline. By expanding and naming different paths that women pursue, I attempt to distinguish their unique experience.

A critical framework exposes the cultural structures that constrain women's choice of major and influence their pursuit of science and mathematics education. Rather than simply examining these factors and labeling them as deficiencies in women, or worse, ignoring the presence of sexist structures and seeing women's choice to leave science as about intrinsic interests, a critical view reveals the constraints and proposes ways to alter disciplinary practice and policies in science. A critical view rejects the interpretation of a tenth-grade female student's change of intended college major to a nonscience major as a natural choice. Instead, this finding suggests the need for more information about the gendered norms and cultural features restricting her choice. Feminist and critical approaches adopt a commitment to liberating people from constricting ideologies.

Feminist and critical inquiry also seeks to reinterpret existing data from a new perspective. This reanalysis can also aim to identify where data do not fit received theory. For example, Carol Gilligan's (1982) ground-breaking work on women's moral development demonstrated that women did not fit Kohlberg's model of moral development that was assumed to be universal. Gilligan's work exposed the distortions of developmental theory and challenged the invisibility of women in theorizing and research. Later, Belenky, Clinchy, Goldberger, and Tarule's (1986) work in cognitive development provided both an oppositional theory to the status quo and a new way to conduct research.

The adoption of a critical and feminist perspective influences the implications of research. In fact, perhaps the crux of what makes research critical is consideration of the question: "Research to what end?" Research conducted in this tradition has the responsibility to connect findings to social transformation and to illuminate, among other things, women's subordination and the pervasiveness of gendered social norms. In sum, critical work seeks to produce greater awareness of the complexity of situations, question the status quo, promote advocacy, and empower those involved to change as well as to understand the world. We should hope that all educational research contributes to such noble social goals.

Where This Research Has Taken Me. My personal experiences of conforming to gendered norms and abandoning my interest in science led me to the topic of women in science. Although my ability to apply a critical perspective was limited by my use of an existing national database comprising traditional, individual-level variables, this study revealed significant gender and racial-ethnic differences in the factors associated with persistence in science education and indicated personal and structural conditions that contributed to women's and students of color's retention in science from eighth grade to postsecondary education. These data offered statistically significant, highly generalizable findings, and clues regarding differential participation rates. However, they did little to expand my understanding of women's experiences in science education and the oppressive structures that persist in maintaining the status quo.

Subsequent to my quantitative research, I completed an in-depth, ethnographic study of women's experiences in science and examined the cultural features in undergraduate science from women students' perspective. This qualitative project provided further opportunities to frame my questions from the point of view of women and to more thoroughly examine the gender stereotypes and sociocultural features of undergraduate science that need to change to make the male-dominated STEM fields less hostile to girls and women.

Conclusion

Adopting a critical and feminist theoretical framework provided me the opportunity to take into account my personal experience and to use this to think differently about educational research and identify and examine the normative problems of traditional quantitative research on women in science. Critical and feminists frames are vitally important to revealing the deficiencies in quantitative projects that seek to understand women in comparison to men, and that rely on traditional positivist methodologies to understand complex social problems. The central themes of critical theory and feminist approaches offer important insights into a more comprehensive examination of the status and condition of girls and women in science education with the aim of promoting action to eliminate constraints and change repressive structures. Given the recent policy of the U.S. government to legislate the scientific method in the realm of educational research, the prominent role of governmental agencies in funding research on science education, and the access to and success of historically underrepresented students in STEM fields, it is especially important to assert methodological diversity and keep critical and feminist research approaches vital to educational research. By supporting critical and feminist perspectives we increase our potential for illuminating where we are and where we want to be in advancing women in science.

References

Ad Council. "Girls Go Tech—It's Her Future. Do the Math." 2002. http://www.adcouncil.org. Accessed Feb. 8, 2007.

Astin, A. W., Tsui, L., and Avalos, J. *Degree Attainment Rates at American Colleges and Universities: Effects on Race, Gender, and Institutional Type.* Los Angeles: University of California, Higher Education Research Institute, 1996.

Belenky, M. F., Clinchy, B. M., Goldberger, N. R., and Tarule, J. M. *Women's Ways of Knowing: The Development of Self, Voice, and Mind.* New York: Basic Books, 1986.

Davis, C., and Associates. *The Equity Equation: Fostering the Advancement of Women in the Sciences, Mathematics, and Engineering.* San Francisco: Jossey-Bass, 1996.

Gilligan, C. *In a Different Voice.* Cambridge, Mass.: Harvard University Press, 1982.

Hanson, S. L. *Lost Talent: Women in the Sciences.* Philadelphia: Temple University Press, 1996.

Harding, S. *Feminism and Methodology.* Bloomington: Indiana University Press, 1987.

Huang, G., Taddese, N., and Walter, E. *Entry and Persistence of Women and Minorities in College Science and Engineering Education.* NCES 2000–601. Washington, D.C.: National Center for Education Statistics, 2000.

Kinzie, J. "Distinguishing Women Science, Mathematics, and Engineering Majors and Non-Majors." Paper presented at the American Educational Research Association annual meeting, Montreal, Canada, 1999.

Kubanek, A. W., and Waller, M. "Women's Confidence in Science: Problematic Notions Around Young Women's Career and Life Choices." *Journal of Women and Minorities in Science and Engineering,* 1995, 2, 243–253.

Lather, P. *Getting Smart: Feminist Research and Pedagogy Within/in the Postmodern.* New York: Routledge, 1991.

Lather, P. "Critical Frames in Educational Research: Feminist and Post-Structural Perspectives." *Theory into Practice,* 1992, *31*(2), 87–99.

Lincoln, Y. S., and Guba, E. G. *Naturalistic Inquiry.* Thousand Oaks, Calif.: Sage, 1985.

Maple, S. A., and Stage, F. K. "Influences on the Choice of Math/Science Major by Gender and Ethnicity." *American Educational Research Journal,* 1991, *28*(1), 37–60.

National Center for Education Statistics. *Digest of Education Statistics, 1999.* Washington, D.C.: U.S. Department of Education, Office of Educational Research and Improvement, 2000.

National Center for Education Statistics. *Digest of Education Statistics, 2005.* NCES 2006-030. Washington, D.C.: U.S. Department of Education, Office of Educational Research and Improvement, 2006.

National Science Foundation. *Women and Science.* Arlington, Va.: Author, 1997.

Nielsen, J. M. "Introduction." In J. Nielsen (ed.), *Feminist Research Methods: Exemplary Readings in the Social Sciences.* Boulder, Colo.: Westview Press, 1990.

Oakes, J. *Lost Talent: The Underrepresentation of Women, Minorities, and Disabled Persons in Science.* Skokie, Ill.: Rand McNally, 1990.

Reinharz, S. *Feminist Methods in Social Research.* New York: Oxford University Press, 1992.

Sax, L. J., Astin, A. W., Korn, W. S., and Mahoney, K. M. *The American Freshman: National Norms for 1998.* Los Angeles: University of California, Higher Education Research Institute, 1998.

Scott, J. "Gender: A Useful Category of Historical Analysis." In C. G. Heilbrun and N. K. Miller (eds.), *Gender and the Politics of History.* New York: Columbia University Press, 1988.

Selingo, J. "Science-Oriented Campuses Strive to Attract More Women." *Chronicle of Higher Education,* Feb. 20, 1998, pp. A53–A54.

Seymour, E. "Tracking the Processes of Change in U.S. Undergraduate Education in Science, Mathematics, Engineering, and Technology." *Science Education,* 2001, *86*(1), 79–105.

Seymour, E., and Hewitt, N. M. *Talking About Leaving: Why Undergraduates Leave the Sciences.* Boulder, Colo.: Westview Press, 1997.

Thom, M. *Balancing the Equation: Where Are the Women and Girls in Science, Engineering, and Technology?* New York: National Council for Research on Women, 2001.

Yoder, J. D., and Kahn, A. "Working Toward an Inclusive Psychology of Women." *American Psychologist,* 1993, *48*(7), 846–850.

JILLIAN KINZIE is associate director of the NSSE Institute for Effective Educational Practice at the Indiana University Center for Postsecondary Research.

8

Most traditional models, frameworks, and findings that apply to the majority of students and faculty do not adequately apply to important subpopulations. The recommendations here will help researchers become more sensitive to the nuances among various educational subgroups, and to pay more attention to outliers.

Moving from Probabilities to Possibilities: Tasks for Quantitative Criticalists

Frances K. Stage

In this chapter I briefly summarize the intent of this book, and discuss some technical reasons why probabilistic research, in the ways it is often conducted using traditional assumptions, masks the experiences of many of the processes in education. I revisit the task of a quantitative criticalist and argue that we should come together across viewpoints in our questioning and in our quest for answers. I close with recommendations for those who wish to incorporate critical perspectives into their own quantitative work and for those who wish to read quantitative work with an open mind about what they might find.

A Brief Review

The authors included in this book came to conduct the work described here independently and in a variety of ways. Each of us has conducted studies using emergent perspectives at various times in our careers. A few of us began our research careers twenty or thirty years ago and initially conducted only quantitative research—much of our work continues in that tradition. At least one of us seeks knowledge primarily from emergent paradigms. Others, more recently minted Ph.D.s, move freely back and forth between paradigms. Yet all of us have come to believe that we can answer some of our most compelling and critical questions using quantitative methods.

New Directions for Institutional Research, no. 133, Spring 2007 © Wiley Periodicals, Inc.
Published online in Wiley InterScience (www.interscience.wiley.com) • DOI: 10.1002/ir.207

In the preceding chapters we presented examples of our critical quantitative research, but we also discussed how we came to believe that our critical questions needed to be answered through quantitative analysis. The topics addressed by quantitative criticalists range across implementing federal, state, and institutional policy; carrying out institutional practices (Parker, 2005); applying accepted theories and measures (Nora and Cabrera, 1996; Stage, Hurtado, Braxton, and St. John, 2001); and conducting standard research practices (Teranishi, 2005).

In Chapter One I enumerated two tasks for quantitative criticalists. The first was *to use data to represent educational processes and outcomes on a large scale to reveal inequities and to identify social or institutional perpetuation of systematic inequities in such processes and outcomes.* Research focusing on this task has been ongoing for the past several years. Yet in Robert Teranishi's chapter, we learn that some of our work in this realm is fraught with conceptualizations that are flawed and that mask inequities for Asian Americans. His work contains lessons for all of us and raises additional concerns about our conceptions of other groups, like Latino students, or even non-mainstream white students, such as working-class rural students. Clearly, we can do more here.

The second task was *to question the models, measures, and analytic practices of quantitative research in order to offer competing models, measures, and analytic practices that better describe experiences of those who have not been adequately represented.* This task too has been "visited" in our research, but real work and change seem more elusive. For example, two of the authors in this volume, Sylvia Hurtado and Deborah Carter, together and independently have spent much of their careers questioning and refining concepts and measures related to student learning and development (Hurtado and Carter, 1997). Two other scholars, Amaury Nora and Alberto Cabrera, have spent much of their careers challenging and expanding conceptualizations of college student persistence and satisfaction (Nora and Cabrera, 1996).

Recently, Estela Bensimon (forthcoming) finds the uniformity of higher education research to be problematic, particularly the use of few models and the lack of conceptual challenges in our work. She critiques higher education research for distancing itself from the situations it studies and reminds us that as scholars our task is to question the work of our intellectual "ancestors." She proposes a new kind of research where institutional stakeholders ask the questions, collect the data, and analyze and ponder the meaning of the results alongside educational researchers.

Another reason for reconsidering our research techniques stems from the nature of probabilistic analysis. In higher education research we often use finely honed causal models to analyze data. Quantitative analysis is a probability game where the majority rules. As we analyze data in large mixed groups, we learn about the majority but little about those on the margins—whether it is the students at risk of dropping out, faculty unlikely to achieve tenure, or underperforming academic departments. The reality of statistical significance is such that even if as much as 10 to 15 percent of our sample has a noteworthy experience that produces a positive outcome, the experience would likely be statistically insignificant in an analysis. Unless we believe that all college students (or faculty or institutions) are alike, our large-scale pooled sample quantitative analysis is senseless in many cases. Usually, we would be better off knowing more about the 10 to 15 percent whose experience differs from the norm.

In my research career, my students and I have conducted myriad analyses of causal models using large national data sets (discussed in Chapter One). Using widely accepted models and controlling for sample size, disaggregating analysis invariably led to conceptual modeling problems. Although most models work very well for some groups, only a few work well for various combinations of gender and racial or ethnic groups. In nearly every case we saw drops in numbers of significant variables accompanied by lower explained variance. Inclusion of socioeconomic status can also result in such variation. These results meant that for students of many underrepresented groups, elements of many current models used in higher education research are misspecified (in other words, wrong) and possibly our measures are wrong as well. For example, what means social integration for you may not mean social integration for me—so measures of social integration that work for me are likely to be wrong for you.

The bad news is that the world is not the same and things are not as simple as they once were. Our baseline of knowledge is no longer adequate for the rapidly changing world that we live in. The good news is that these problems define our work for us . . . and there is plenty to do.

Possibilities

A few years ago I had dinner with friends, one of whom was a higher education doctoral student enrolled in a well-known program. The conversation turned to research, and the student asked how I could persist in testing quantitative models—didn't I know that I was setting a bad example for my doctoral students? I replied that I would continue testing quantitative models that helped me demonstrate that the assumptions on which many quantitative models were founded do not "work" for nontraditional students. Nevertheless, I was taken aback by her question. I wondered how her faculty could persist in teaching inquiry in such a divisive manner.

As long as researchers with differing perspectives are taught to believe that other approaches are worthless, we will remain where we are, making only incremental gains in knowledge. We will continue to read the work of others who think the way we do, use similar conceptual frameworks and models, and use the same data analysis techniques. We will be reassured when their findings are exactly the ones that we have found over the years and alarmed and skeptical if they are not.

Most of what we study with quantitative approaches is probability based. As quantitative researchers, most of us have in the past and possibly continue now to report the most likely experiences for the samples we study, whether high school students aspiring to attend college, college students, faculty, institutions, or departments. Future work that is much needed entails reports of less likely experiences, parts of our sample that are unusual, and smaller samples that refute our "accepted truths." In other words, we need to pay more attention to outliers.

Probability-based analysis is in most instances no longer useful for large aggregated groups given the amount of research we have already conducted in that manner. Most people who analyze data in higher education have moved beyond reporting averages that describe institutions or processes en masse. Today, most data analysts and researchers are focused on solving problems: how to do more with lower budgets and more students or how to increase first- to second-year retention at a given institution. Considering the level of detail that we need to know about particular people in particular contexts or about particular situations, narrower focus is the answer. The value of the increased sophistication of institutional and national data sets is that we can use them to make meaningful distinctions in data and conduct our analyses disaggregated into meaningful groups whether the groups are a set of academic departments that share similar characteristics or low-income students whose parents did not attend college.

So, in light of these issues, how do we move forward in an evolutionary process? Three tasks are before us: we must move beyond our comfort zones and read more broadly; we must question our assumptions, models, methods, and measures; and we must study institutions and people in the context of their particular circumstances.

Moving Beyond Our Comfort Zones to Read More Broadly. The work of qualitative researchers can serve to provide us with ideas about populations to be studied, constructs to be added to models, and new ways of measuring old constructs. Bensimon and her colleagues visit college campuses to learn what qualitative measures would be of interest and use to faculty and administrators. Just as puzzling findings in quantitative work can provide topics of exploration for both quantitative and qualitative researchers, similar inspiration can be found in qualitative research findings. Sometimes qualitative study sheds light on problematic assumptions of quantitative models.

One way to accomplish broader thinking is to engage approaches that combine both qualitative and quantitative methods and that capitalize on the strengths of both types of researchers. Some argue that the use of mixed approaches is fraught with problems. But much research is fraught with problems, and those of us who witnessed the beginnings of qualitative and naturalistic research approaches in education in the late seventies and early eighties remember that painful lessons have always been part of the development of creative new ways of learning. Mixed-approach studies can provide the means for critical questioning of our results so that we can learn at deeper levels. Such study can be conducted alone or with a colleague whose expertise differs from one's own, prompting discussions that provide opportunities for expansive thinking. Such studies will also serve to help us modify existing models and approaches.

Questioning Our Assumptions, Models, Methods, and Measures. One of my wise graduate students observed that our finely developed causal models created a certain level of complacency with which we approached our studies. Already knowing much of what we will find, we do not think beyond those expectations in designing our research. We must begin our research conceptualizations with more questions and interrogate our models more closely. In the late 1990s Braxton, Sullivan, and Johnson (1997) conducted a metanalysis of testable propositions in the Tinto model, based on the outcomes of two decades of research. They found strong support for few of the major causal paths and little more than moderate support for only half the others. Yet use of that model has increased exponentially in the decade since (Bensimon, forthcoming).

Next our task turns to methods and measures. Problems here are likely more insidious than problems with the model. Often simple institutional data and responses to standard questionnaires are used as proxy measures for complex constructs, such as the common use of grade point average as a measure of academic integration. Such issues can undermine any good model. Finally, many of us regularly test models in our work, but when we find good reason to question a model by demonstrating the weaknesses we should also be willing to pose an alternative.

Finally, we need to use our minds well. The study of higher education is an insular enterprise. We are a group with few degrees of separation between ourselves and our colleagues. Many of us can see a name and recall two or three recent publications authored by that individual. Although this insular knowledge carries with it a certain comfort and surety, it also restricts us in notions of correctness and authority. We look to the same names for answers that might not work given changes described earlier. We adopt approaches to research that are guided by reservation and conventional wisdoms.

Studying Institutions and People in the Context of Their Particular Circumstances. The world of higher education is rapidly changing—from federal support to institutions, to presidential leadership style, to characteristics of new students. With these changes our baselines of knowledge require shifts and modifications. When populations differ, separate analyses are needed. Differences in peoples' experiences require closer focus on racial or ethnic groups. Furthermore, we must push to examine within racial groups . . . exploring difference and resisting the temptation to make blanket comparisons across groups. Even within groups, socioeconomic status for African American and white students and country of origin and immigrant status for Latino and Asian American students have uncovered significant differences.

Work reported in the chapters in this volume can be viewed as examples for those who seek to move their own research agendas beyond the expected. In all areas of educational study, work that pushes the boundaries is needed. Moreover, such quantitative interrogation is critically important given increasing federal skepticism about the relevance of qualitative research to educational policymaking. We need more approaches that capitalize on information provided by both qualitative and quantitative approaches. We must put all our resources into critical higher education work—all our approaches and our variety of conceptualizations have a contribution to make. As *quantitative criticalists* we invite you to join in our questioning.

References

Bensimon, E. "The Underestimated Significance of Practitioner Knowledge in the Scholarship on Student Success." *Review of Higher Education,* forthcoming.

Braxton, J., Sullivan, A., and Johnson, R. "Appraising Tinto's Theory of College Student Departure." In J. Smart (ed.), *Higher Education: Handbook of Theory and Research* (pp. 107–164). New York: Agathon, 1997.

Hurtado, S., and Carter, D. F. "Effects of College Transition and Perceptions of the Campus Racial Climate on Latino College Students' Sense of Belonging." *Sociology of Education,* 1997, 70, 324–345.

Nora, A., and Cabrera, A. "The Role of Perceptions of Prejudice and Discrimination on the Adjustment of Minority Students in College." *Journal of Higher Education,* 1996, 67(2), 119–148.

Parker, T. "Broken Promises of Opportunity? Reducing Remediation at CUNY." Paper presented at the Association for the Study of Higher Education, Philadelphia, Nov. 2005.

Stage, F. K., Hurtado, S., Braxton, J., and St. John, E. "Limitations of Probabilistic Research in the Study of College Students." Paper presented at the Association for the Study of Higher Education, Richmond, Va., Nov. 2001.

Teranishi, R. *Normative Approaches to Policy Research in Education: Implications for Asian Americans and Pacific Islanders.* New York: College Board, 2005.

FRANCES K. STAGE is professor of administration, leadership, and technology in the Steinhardt School at New York University and a former Senior Fellow at the National Science Foundation.

INDEX

IR127   **Survey Research: Emerging Issues**
Paul D. Umbach
Demands for accountability are forcing colleges and universities to conduct
more high-quality surveys to gauge institutional effectiveness. New
technologies are improving survey implementation as well as researchers'
ability to effectively analyze data. This volume examines these emerging
issues in a rapidly changing environment and highlights lessons learned
from past research.
ISBN: 0-7879-8329-2

IR126   **Enhancing Alumni Research: European and American Perspectives**
David J. Weerts, Javier Vidal
The increasing globalization of higher education has made it easy to
compare problems, goals, and tools associated with conducting alumni
research worldwide. This research is also being used to learn about the
impact, purposes, and successes of higher education. This volume will help
institutional leaders use alumni research to respond to the increasing
demands of state officials, accrediting agencies, employers, prospective
students, parents, and the general public.
ISBN: 0-7879-8228-8

IR125   **Minority Retention: What Works?**
Gerald H. Gaither
Examines some of the best policies, practices, and procedures to achieve
greater diversity and access, while controlling costs and maintaining quality.
Looks at institutions that are majority-serving, tribal, Hispanic-serving, and
historically black. Emphasizes that the key to retention is in the professional
commitment of faculty and staff to student-centered efforts, and includes
practical ideas adaptable to different institutional goals.
ISBN: 0-7879-7974-0

IR124   **Unique Campus Contexts: Insights for Research and Assessment**
Jason E. Lane, M. Christopher Brown II
Summarizes what we know about professional schools, transnational campuses,
proprietary schools, religious institutions, and corporate universities. As more
students take advantage of these specialized educational environments,
conducting meaningful research becomes a challenge. The authors argue for the
importance of educational context and debunk the one-size-fits-all approach to
assessment, evaluation, and research. Effective institutional measures of
inquiry, benchmarks, and indicators must be congruent with the mission,
population, and function of each unique campus context.
ISBN: 0-7879-7973-2

IR123   **Successful Strategic Planning**
Michael J. Dooris, John M. Kelley, James F. Trainer
Explains the value of strategic planning in higher education to improve
conditions and meet missions (hiring better faculty, recruiting stronger
students, upgrading facilities, improving programs, acquiring resources), and
what planning tools and methodologies have been used at various campuses.
Goes beyond the activity of planning to investigate successful ways to implement
and infuse strategic plans throughout the organization. Case studies from
various campuses show different ways to achieve success.
ISBN: 0-7879-7792-6

IR122   Assessing Character Outcomes in College
Jon C. Dalton, Terrence R. Russell, Sally Kline
Examines several perspectives on the role of higher education in developing
students' character, and illustrates approaches to defining and assessing
character outcomes. Moral, civic, ethical, and spiritual development are key
aspects of students' growth and experience in college, so how can educators
encourage good values and assess their impact?
ISBN: 0-7879-7791-8

IR121   Overcoming Survey Research Problems
Stephen R. Porter
As demand for survey research has increased, survey response rates have
decreased. This volume examines an array of survey research problems and
best practices, from both the literature and field practitioners, to provide
solutions to increase response rates while controlling costs. Discusses
administering longitudinal studies, doing surveys on sensitive topics such as
student drug and alcohol use, and using new technologies for survey
administration.
ISBN: 0-7879-7477-3

IR120   Using Geographic Information Systems in Institutional Research
Daniel Teodorescu
Exploring the potential of geographic information systems (GIS) applications
in higher education administration, this issue introduces IR professionals and
campus administrators to a powerful presentation and analysis tool. Chapters
explore the benefits of working with the spatial component of data in
recruitment, admissions, facilities, alumni development, and other areas, with
examples of actual GIS applications from several higher education institutions.
ISBN: 0-7879-7281-9

IR119   Maximizing Revenue in Higher Education
F. King Alexander, Ronald G. Ehrenberg
This volume presents edited versions of some of the best articles from a forum
on institutional revenue generation sponsored by the Cornell Higher Education
Research Institute. The chapters provide different perspectives on revenue
generation and how institutions are struggling to find an appropriate balance
between meeting public expectations and maximizing private market forces.
The insights provided about options and alternatives will enable campus
leaders, institutional researchers, and policymakers to better understand
evolving patterns in public and private revenue reliance.
ISBN: 0-7879-7221-5

IR118   Studying Diverse Institutions: Contexts, Challenges, and Considerations
M. Christopher Brown II, Jason E. Lane
This volume examines the contextual and methodological issues pertaining to
studying diverse institutions (including women's colleges, tribal colleges, and
military academies), and provides effective and useful approaches for higher
education administrators, institutional researchers and planners, policymakers,
and faculty seeking to better understand students in postsecondary education.
It also offers guidelines to asking the right research questions, employing the
appropriate research design and methods, and analyzing the data with respect
to the unique institutional contexts.
ISBN: 0-7879-6990-7

IR117   Unresolved Issues in Conducting Salary-Equity Studies
Robert K. Toutkoushian
Chapters discuss the issues surrounding how to use faculty rank, seniority, and experience as control variables in salary-equity studies. Contributors review the challenges of conducting a salary-equity study for nonfaculty administrators and staff—who constitute the majority of employees, even in academic institutions—and examine the advantages and disadvantages of using hierarchical linear modeling to measure pay equity. They present a case-study approach to illustrate the political and practical challenges that researchers often face when conducting a salary-equity study for an institution. This is a companion volume to *Conducting Salary-Equity Studies: Alternative Approaches to Research* (IR115).
ISBN: 0-7879-6863-3

IR116   **Reporting Higher Education Results: Missing Links in the Performance Chain**
Joseph C. Burke, Henrick P. Minassians
The authors review performance reporting's coverage, content, and customers, they examine in depth the reporting indicators, types, and policy concerns, and they compare them among different states' reports. They highlight weaknesses in our current performance reporting—such as a lack of comparable indicators for assessing the quality of undergraduate education—and make recommendations about how to best use and improve performance information.
ISBN: 0-7879-6336-4

IR115   **Conducting Salary-Equity Studies: Alternative Approaches to Research**
Robert K. Toutkoushian
Synthesizing nearly 30 years of research on salary equity from the field of economics and the experiences of past studies, this issue launches an important dialogue between scholars and institutional researchers on the methodology and application of salary-equity studies in today's higher education institutions. The first of a two-volume set on the subject, it also bridges the gap between academic research and the more pragmatic statistical and political considerations in real-life institutional salary studies.
ISBN: 0-7879-6335-6

IR114   **Evaluating Faculty Performance**
Carol L. Colbeck
This issue brings new insights to faculty work and its assessment in light of reconsideration of faculty work roles, rapid technological change, increasing bureaucratization of the core work of higher education, and public accountability for performance. Exploring successful methods that individuals, institutions, and promotion and tenure committees are using for evaluations of faculty performance for career development, this issue is an indispensable guide to academic administrators and institutional researchers involved in the faculty evaluation process.
ISBN: 0-7879-6334-8

IR113   **Knowledge Management: Building a Competitive Advantage in Higher Education**
Andreea M. Serban, Jing Luan
Provides a comprehensive discussion of knowledge management, covering its theoretical, practical, and technological aspects with an emphasis on their relevance for applications in institutional research. Chapters examine the theoretical basis and impact of data mining; discuss the role of institutional research in customer relationship management; and provide a framework for the integration of institutional research within the larger context of organization

learning. With a synopsis of technologies that support knowledge management and an exploration of future developments in this field, this volume assists institutional researchers and analysts in taking advantage of the opportunities of knowledge management and addressing its challenges.
ISBN: 0-7879-6291-0

IR112   **Balancing Qualitative and Quantitative Information for Effective Decision Support**
Richard D. Howard, Kenneth W. Borland Jr.
Establishes methods for integration of numeric data and its contextual application. With theoretical and practical examples, contributors explore the techniques and realities of creating, communicating, and using balanced decision support information. Chapters discuss the critical role of measurement in building institutional quality; examples of conceptual and theoretical frameworks and their application for the creation of evaluation information; and methods of communicating data and information in relation to its decision support function.
ISBN: 0-7879-5796-8

IR111   **Higher Education as Competitive Enterprise: When Markets Matter**
Robert Zemsky, Susan Shaman, Daniel B. Shapiro
Offers a comprehensive history of the development and implementation of Collegiate Results Instrument (CRI), a tool for mapping the connection between market forces and educational outcomes in higher education. Chapters detail the methods that CRI uses to help institutions to remain value centered by becoming market smart.
ISBN: 0-7879-5795-X

IR110   **Measuring What Matters: Competency-Based Learning Models in Higher Education**
Richard Voorhees
An analysis of the findings of the National Postsecondary Education Cooperative project on data and policy implications of national skill standards, this issue provides researchers, faculty, and academic administrators with the tools needed to deal effectively with the emerging competency-based initiatives.
ISBN: 0-7879-1411-8

IR109   **The Student Ratings Debate: Are They Valid? How Can We Best Use Them?**
Michael Theall, Philip C. Abrami, Lisa A. Mets
Presents a thorough analysis of the use of student evaluations of teaching for summative decisions and discusses the ongoing controversies, emerging research, and dissenting opinions on their utility and validity. Summarizes the role of student ratings as tools for instructional improvement, as evidence for promotion and tenure decisions, as the means for student course selection, as a criterion of program effectiveness, and as the continuing focus of active research and intensive discussion.
ISBN: 0-7879-5756-9

IR108   **Collaboration Between Student Affairs and Institutional Researchers to Improve Institutional Effectiveness**
J. Worth Pickering, Gary R. Hanson
Defines the unique aspects of student affairs research, including its role in responding to assessment mandates and accreditation agencies, its use of student development theory in formulating research questions, the value of qualitative methods it employs, and the potential contribution it can make to institutional decision making.
ISBN: 0-7879-5727-5

IR107   Understanding the College Choice of Disadvantaged Students
         Alberto F. Cabrera, Steven M. La Nasa
         Examines the college-choice decision of minority and disadvantaged students
         and suggests avenues to help promote access and improve participation.
         Explores the influence of family and high school variables as well as racial and
         ethnic differences on college-choice.
         ISBN: 0-7879-5439-X

IR106   **Analyzing Costs in Higher Education: What Institutional Researchers
         Need to Know**
         Michael F. Middaugh
         Presents both the conceptual and practical information that will give researchers
         solid grounding in selecting the best approach to cost analysis. Offers an
         overview of cost studies covering basic issues and beyond, from a review of
         definitions of expenditure categories and rules of financial reporting to a
         discussion of a recent congressionally mandated study of higher education costs.
         ISBN: 0-7879-5437-3

NEW DIRECTIONS FOR INSTITUTIONAL RESEARCH
Order Form
SUBSCRIPTIONS AND SINGLE ISSUES

DISCOUNTED BACK ISSUES:

Use this form to receive **20% off** all back issues of New Directions for Institutional Research. All single issues priced at **$23.20** (normally $29.00)

TITLE	ISSUE NO.	ISBN
_____	_____	_____
_____	_____	_____
_____	_____	_____

Call 888-378-2537 or see mailing instructions below. When calling, mention the promotional code, JB7ND, to receive your discount.

SUBSCRIPTIONS: *(1 year, 4 issues)*

☐ New Order   ☐ Renewal

U.S.	☐ Individual: $80	☐ Institutional: $185
Canada/Mexico	☐ Individual: $80	☐ Institutional: $225
All Others	☐ Individual: $104	☐ Institutional: $269

Call 888-378-2537 or see mailing and pricing instructions below. Online subscriptions are available at www.interscience.wiley.com.

Copy or detach page and send to:

John Wiley & Sons, Journals Dept, 5th Floor
989 Market Street, San Francisco, CA 94103-1741

Order Form can also be faxed to: 888-481-2665

Issue/Subscription Amount: $ _____
Shipping Amount: $ _____
(for single issues only—subscription prices include shipping)
Total Amount: $ _____

SHIPPING CHARGES:

SURFAC	Domestic	Canadian
First Item	$5.00	$6.00
Each Add'l Item	$3.00	$1.50

(No sales tax for U.S. subscriptions. Canadian residents, add GST for subscription orders. Individual rate subscriptions must be paid by personal check or credit card. Individual rate subscriptions may not be resold as library copies.)

☐ Payment enclosed (U.S. check or money order only. All payments must be in U.S. dollars.)

☐ VISA ☐ MC ☐ Amex # _____ Exp. Date _____

Card Holder Name _____ Card Issue # _____

Signature_____ Day Phone _____

☐ Bill Me (U.S. institutional orders only. Purchase order required.)

Purchase order # _____
Federal Tax ID13559302   GST 89102 8052

Name_____

Address _____

Phone _____ E-mail _____

JB7ND

Get Online Access to
New Directions for Institutional Research

New Directions for Institutional Research is available through Wiley InterScience, the dynamic online content service from John Wiley & Sons. Visit our Web site and enjoy a range of extremely useful features:

WILEY INTERSCIENCE ALERTS
Content Alerts: Receive tables of contents alerts via e-mail as soon as a new issue is online.
Profiled Alerts: Set up your own e-mail alerts based on personal queries, keywords, and other parameters.

WILEY
InterScience®
www.interscience.wiley.com
Discover something great

QUICK AND POWERFUL SEARCHING
Browse and Search functions are designed to lead you to the information you need quickly and easily. Whether searching by title, keyword, or author, your results will point directly to the journal article, book chapter, encyclopedia entry or database you seek.

PERSONAL HOME PAGE
Store and manage Wiley InterScience Alerts, searches, and links to key journals and articles.

MOBILEEDITION™
Download table of contents and abstracts to your PDA every time you synchronize.

CROSSREF®
Move seamlessly from a reference in a journal article to the cited journal articles, which may be located on a different server and published by a different publisher.

LINKS
Navigate to and from indexing and abstracting services.

For more information about online access, please contact us at: North,Central, and South America: 1-800-511-3989, uscs-wis@wiley.com
All other regions: (+44) (0) 1243-843-345, cs-wis@wiley.co.uk

www.interscience.wiley.com